WRITING ABOUT TRAVEL

Second Edition

Morag Campbell

A & C Black · London

To the memory of my father,
James Campbell

Second edition 1995
First edition 1989
A & C Black (Publishers) Limited
35 Bedford Row, London WC1R 4JH

© 1995, 1989 Morag Campbell

ISBN 0–7136–4174–6

A CIP catalogue record for this book
is available from the British Library.

Cover illustration by Russell Walker

Typeset by Florencetype Ltd, Stoodleigh, Devon
Printed in Great Britain by Redwood Books,
Trowbridge, Wilts.

Contents

Preface to the second edition

By definition, travel is never a static subject (except when stuck in a traffic jam or an airport strike) but since the publication of the first edition of *Writing About Travel* there have been some momentous changes in the travel world, not least the opening of the Channel Tunnel. The name Yugoslavia has disappeared from our maps, East and West Germany have been united, and the former USSR has metamorphosed into a Commonwealth of Independent States. On a less dramatic scale, the opening of Buckingham Palace to the public by the Queen, cheap flights to the Far East, the increasing ease with which one can get married abroad, swim with dolphins or take up snowboarding rather than skiing, all spell new experiences and writing opportunities for those who love to travel. The world may be shrinking, but the scope for exploring is increasing, as, too, are the number of magazines and newspapers carrying travel articles as a regular feature.

Introduction

To travel to far away places and to be paid to write about your experiences is most people's idea of heaven: to be a travel writer opens doors to privileges, encounters and insights which often only the very fortunate or the very wealthy can enjoy.

Not everyone who has caught the travel bug exorcises it by writing about it. Some assuage it by becoming pilots or air stewards, travel couriers or perhaps by joining the marketing department of an international company. But this book is written for those people who long to put their experiences down on paper. There are innumerable shades of travel experiences, which, if properly presented and recounted with style, a wide public is eager to read.

Writing about travel is not an impossible dream; this book is intended to show you how to make that dream come true. The rest is up to you.

1
Motives

It is impossible to take a train or an aeroplane without having a fantasy of oneself as a Quest Hero starting off in search of an enchanted princess or the waters of life.

W. H. Auden

Not since the 1920s and 1930s, when books like *The Valleys of the Assassins*, *Forbidden Journey* and *News from Tartary* were so popular, has there been so much interest in reading about other people's travels. Perhaps the feeling that the world is changing so rapidly, that it is being reshaped around us and will never be the same again, makes us want to capture it in print now.

Why do people travel? Many see it as the ultimate escape, although Horace claimed, 'They change their climate, not their souls, who rush across the sea'. Some people have an inborn need to keep on the move, a primal wanderlust, and in his book *The Songlines*, Bruce Chatwin even claims this is our natural state. Most of us, however, aren't in a permanent state of wanderlust but feel the urge to get away occasionally, which is described aptly by the nineteenth-century Russian philosopher Alexander Herzen:

> After living a long time in one place and in the same rut, I feel that for a certain time it is enough. I must refresh myself with other horizons and other faces. . . . There are people who prefer to get away inwardly, some with the help of a powerful imagination and an ability to abstract themselves from their surroundings (for this a special endowment is needed bordering on genius and insanity), some with the help of opium or alcohol. Russians, for instance, will have a drinking-bout for a week or two, and then go back to their homes and duties. I prefer shifting my whole body to shifting my brain, and going round the world to letting my head go round. Perhaps it is because I have a bad head after too much to drink.

It is particularly interesting to find out what motivates well-known travel writers. Colin Thubron, one of the best-known of contemporary travel writers, is a compulsive traveller 'as restless with people as I am with places . . . a sort of refusal to settle for what the world seems to offer, combined with a belief that there must be something else. Even if I found myself in paradise I'd feel the need to move on.'

Evelyn Waugh, who maintained that he fought in the Second World War for the freedom to travel, certainly gives the impression in his books that he travelled to escape the weather. In his first travel book, *Labels*, he writes of the London winter from which he was so anxious to escape in very depressing terms:

> In February 1929 almost every cause was present which can contribute to human discomfort. London was lifeless and numb. . . . People shrank, in those days, from the icy contact of a cocktail glass . . . and crept stiff as automata from their draughty taxis into the nearest tube railway station, where they stood, pressed together for warmth, coughing and sneezing among the evening papers.

Years later, in 1958, he again decided he couldn't endure another British winter but then had the problem of where to go:

> It is not so easy as it was 30 years ago to find a retreat. Tourism and politics have laid waste everywhere. Nor is 55 the best age to travel; too old for the jungle, too young for the beaches, [sic], one must seek refreshment in the spectacle of other people at work, leading lives quite different from one's own.

Having dismissed Jamaica, and India ('full of splendours that must be seen now or perhaps never, but can a man of 55 long endure a regime where wine is prohibited?'), he settled on Africa with 'eyes reopened to the exotic'.

What kind of travel writer are you?

What you are travelling to escape from may dictate the kind of travel writing you succumb to. Escaping from the weather may send you to warmer climates; escaping from boredom may lead you to take part in expeditions, scale mountains, or trek through remote parts of the globe. One of the famous travel writers of the 1930s, Peter Fleming, answered the following advertisement in *The Times* which was to result in his book *Brazilian Adventure*: 'Exploring and sporting expedition under experienced guidance, leaving England June, to explore rivers Central Brazil, if possible ascertain fate Colonel Fawcett.' He maintained that 'four male children out of five start life predisposed in favour of adventure . . . which is really a soft option: adventure has always been a selfish business. They do it because they want to. It suits them; it is their cup of tea.' He even went on to claim that it requires far less courage to be an explorer than to be a chartered accountant. 'The courage which enables you to face the prospect of sitting on a high stool in a smoky town and adding up figures over a period of years is definitely a higher, as well as more useful, sort of courage than any which the explorer may be called on to display.'

Vogue contributors travel for 'the excitement of discovering new places and the pleasure of revisiting old ones'. Dr Johnson wrote, unromantically, that 'The use of travelling is to regulate imagination by reality, and instead of thinking how things may be, to see them as they are', which might well be regarded as a suitable motto for guide book writers. Most of us travel in the hope of enriching our experience of life. The trouble is that, the easier travel may become physically, the less rewarding it gets spiritually. Sharing the Acropolis with the sight and sound of hundreds of other tourists may entitle you to say you have seen the Parthenon, but whether the experience will have enriched or uplifted you is dubious.

Sorting out your priorities – money or prestige?

Once you have sorted out your motives for travel then you will be able to sort out your priorities for writing about travel. Are you content to write on travel as a hobby or would you like to make a full-time living from it? Do you want to write to pay for further travel? To make pin money or a great deal of money? For personal recognition? For the glamour and excitement of travel? For adventure? Or do you want to be a travel writer purely from the need to say 'This is the world as *I* see it: this is the world through *my* eyes'?

Work out whether you are motivated chiefly by ego or money: naturally most people would like to satisfy both, but have to settle for one or the other. Travel writing is an uncertain way of working and only a handful of people ever earn a living purely through travelling and writing. Professional travel writers have to have enormous stamina in order to visit different countries and climates every month, cope with airline schedules, crowded airports, irregular meals, strange and not always palatable food and drink, yet maintain a constant spring of marketable ideas.

You will then have to sort out what kind of traveller you are. Will you travel as a tourist? At heart, are you a nomad, a wanderer, a traveller or a globe-trotter? Travel writers don't like being described as 'tourists', but quite frequently are. Being a tourist on a package tour doesn't debar you from travel writing and, depending on your market, don't forget that an appreciable number of your readers will also be package tourists.

You will have to consider whether you want to travel alone or in company. Colin Thubron, whose book, *Behind the Wall, A Journey through China* won a Thomas Cook Travel Book Award, is emphatic that he would hate to travel with anyone else.

> Had I been travelling in company I would have found my Western-ness continually reaffirmed. I would always have been thinking, 'We are normal, they are peculiar', and trying to understand the environment I had set out to explore would have been much more difficult. If you're on your own people assume you need company – it's very easy to initiate conversations and attract hospitality.

But for numerous other people, having the family along on their travels is an integral part of the story. Remember that as well as the stimulating experiences you will have, boredom and loneliness may assail you abroad, and even travel writers get homesick from time to time. Don't forget, however, that the first rule of success-ful travel writing is 'never be boring, no matter how boring the experience'.

Matching temperament to travel writing

There is also the question of what kind of writing your own temperament suggests. A travel book gives you the opportunity to dwell on your experiences and encounters: in an article many a rewarding encounter has to be confined to a short sentence or excluded altogether because of space constraints. Nor does the author of a personal account need to include details on how to get to Saigon, what the currency exchange rate is, what inoculations and vaccinations you need before you go. The writer of the auto-biographical travel book is – or should be – a free spirit, free certainly of the nitty-gritty details which are often required when writing travel articles for newspapers.

A guide book demands a conscientious approach and consider-able attention to detail – take a look at the *Blue Guides* to see the kind of detailed writing involved. The guide book writer needs enormous patience and perseverance, and you may find that, temperamentally, you may not be suited to writing such a book at all. Even the shortest book involves a long stretch of concentrated work which monopolises your life for months on end and a personal account of a journey or adventure may turn out to be a chore once you are back home. Temperamentally you may be more inclined towards writing travel articles for newspapers, for these are usually short and can be written in a day, or for magazines where the article required seldom exceeds 1500 words.

Do you get more pleasure from passing on interesting information you have acquired along the way, or more satisfaction from writing a description of the world around you and in trying to capture its character in print? Jan Morris doesn't like to be categorised as a writer of travel books (even though her book about Venice is regarded as a modern classic), and claims that when she writes about places 'I write specifically, if you will pardon an insufferable egotism, about their personal relationships, Manhattan or Paris, Rio or Shanghai, with me! ... The act of travel provides a sort of ready-made plot: characters obligingly present themselves for portraiture: one can wander at will in and out of imagination.'

Perhaps Jonathan Raban sums up best why people travel. In *Old Glory*, where he writes about his journey down the Mississippi, he admits he was on a quest 'to find a shape, a meaning to the river, and to life itself.'

2
What Travel
Editors Want

'A bit of a buzz, a bit of pizazz,' claims the travel editor of *The Times*, and certainly it's only when you've read your way through hundreds of flat and pedestrian travel articles that you realise how relatively rare the buzz factor is in the heap of manuscripts submitted every week to travel editors.

'Originality, humour, and a sense of place,' is what the travel editor of *The Daily Telegraph* looks for. 'Freshness and originality and an unusual perspective,' according to her opposite number on *The Times*. 'No hackneyed accounts of springtime in Paris or summer on the Costa.'

Nevertheless, as she concedes, it's more difficult to write about well-known places such as Paris than a little-known destination such as Vietnam. 'Local characters rather than spectacular sunsets, and perhaps even a little criticism.'

You have, of course, to know your market. A little criticism may go down well with *The Times*, but could well be the reason for rejection in less independently-minded publications. Don't, on the other hand, go to the other extreme – avoid syncophantic travel writing at all costs.

'You have to catch my attention right from the first sentence,' is the advice editors frequently give. 'I want to know if it is the type of place that would interest me, whether it's somewhere I'd like to visit.' But hooking the editor's attention isn't enough – the momentum of the journey must drive the article on, something must happen. Blandness can be the death of a travel article. As the travel editor of the *Guardian* says, 'You need a bit of magic. It's not where you've been but how you write about it.'

But even Colin Thubron, one of the leading contemporary travel writers, admits that there is a certain sameness about the world today. 'Over there, as likely as not, everything will be depressingly the same, and a foreign country may merely cast back our own image at us – a little distorted, a little grotesque.'

The American travel writer Bill Bryson has noticed that 'there is an assumption not only among aspiring travel writers but among professionals too, that because they went there and they had a good or an interesting time, that there is something intrinsically interesting about their trip, and that isn't so at all . . . repeating the facts of the journey isn't enough. You are obliged to make your journey interesting enough that it will seize the reader's attention and keep it engaged.'

'It's very easy to fall back on clichéd images in travel writing: there are only so many ways you can describe a mountain, only so many ways you can describe a blue sea. But that's the challenge of it: to bring a freshness to it.'

Freshness yes, naivety no. The first time experience often has a freshness about it that return journeys can never recapture, but cities such as Paris or New York have been so well written about that they seldom lend themselves to the ingenué approach.

Would-be contributors to magazines and newspapers also have to recognise seasonality. There is a time and a season for family holidays, post-Easter breaks, winter sun, and city breaks. The *Guardian*, for instance, tends to use long pieces on remote places in August when the paper is flat. The *Daily Telegraph* works three to four months ahead on travel articles.

The travel editor of the *Daily Express* looks for articles which reflect how ordinary people travel – 'sharply written, with a people landscape', from 350–750 words and wishes more people would write about places in the UK rather than exotic destinations.

It is, rather obviously, necessary to write to the correct length for the publication you have in mind. Submitting a 2000-word article to one of the tabloids is asking for rejection. Study the newspaper or magazine closely for length and style, but bear in mind that in these competitive times a new editor may decree a change of layout, longer or shorter articles.

Travel writing has elements in common with all good writing, and phrases like 'Melancholy rises like a mist from the Seine' linger in the mind whether you read them in a novel or a news report.

John Diamond, a freelance writer and broadcaster who has been a judge of many a travel writing competition, including the *Guardian's*, knows he will find a predictable number of entries describing 'dark clouds looming', and at least a dozen people who believe they have newly coined the phrase 'the warm air hit me like a hot, damp towel round the face' to describe the experience of getting off the plane at Miami airport. To my chagrin, I suspect I was guilty of using this phrase myself after a trip to India.

It's not easy being original, far less avoiding clichés, but when you come across someone who writes 'as rare as rocking horse manure' or uses an inspired phrase like 'Lozeriens use every bit of their pigs but the *oink*', a phrase which appeared in a travel article in the *Daily Telegraph* recently, *that* is originality.

3
Getting Started

You will never be a writer of any kind – novelist, columnist or travel writer – unless you get words down on paper. How you do this is a personal matter. It is quicker if you write fired by inspiration, when it is sometimes impossible to write fast enough to keep up with all the ideas flaring up. Having a deadline helps to concentrate the mind, but if you have neither inspiration nor a deadline, what do you do?

Many writers claim that they sit at their desk and write from 9 to 5 every day, six days a week, come what may, and certainly the more you write the easier it becomes to put words down on paper which express your feelings and emotions about a place, and give each sentence the weight and significance on paper that it has in your head.

It is easy as you commute to work or wash the dishes to write an article in your head; the phrases crowd in easily and one subject flows like water into the next until you have reached the required 750 or 1000 words, a witty ending and full stop.

But of course it isn't nearly so simple, or everyone would be writing, and it is especially hard to keep up the discipline of writing when you have no goal in view. Regard the daily exercise of writing as an apprenticeship to develop your writing skills and make a point of sending off one completed manuscript to an editor each week, or at least one idea. (See chapter 6 for more on submitting travel articles and query letters).

Give yourself goals

Envisage the day when travel editors will ring you up with commissions or ask you for ideas; imagine airlines or public relations companies ringing to invite you to Florida next Thursday or ask if you are free on the 14th for a weekend in Monte Carlo. It is by no means a fantasy – this situation is an everyday occurrence for travel editors and freelance travel writers too. It won't happen to you, however, if they don't know you or your work. Until that happy day arrives, keep it as your goal. By the time you are an established travel writer you won't ever write an article 'on spec' again, as all your work will be specifically commissioned.

To reach this stage, however, you must have examples of your published work to show – the old Catch 22 situation. Success breeds success: the more often you are published, the more often your name appears in print, the more likely you are to find your ideas and suggestions accepted by editors.

Keep an ideas file

You may well object that it is hard to think up enough ideas every week to suggest them to editors, let alone write one travel article a week on spec. A strategy which holds good for all feature writing is especially true of travel writing; keep an ideas file. Buy or acquire as many newspapers and magazines as you can and use them for ideas – ideas, note, and not plagiarism – to compile an 'I could have written that' file. The range of magazines in doctors', dentists' and hospital waiting rooms are often the only aspect of a visit which is bearable. A visit to the hairdresser may later pay for itself with the ideas gleaned from the selection of magazines you are able to study under the dryer. But whether you are visiting the dentist or hairdresser, take a notebook with you. Sometimes a particular magazine can suggest so many ideas that unless you take a note of them as they occur the ideas escape for good.

Revise your ideas file regularly, updating and planning new angles. New magazines and newspapers are constantly appearing on the bookstands. Study their travel columns to see whether your existing ideas could fit their format, or be re-angled to suit their market. Keep a forward diary for ideas which aren't topical at the moment, but could be the basis of future travel articles.

Work out half a dozen ideas and aim to write about them at the rate of one a week. Since the average newspaper travel article is about 500–700 words, they needn't be long, and it is a considerable discipline keeping the subject matter down to this length. Magazines, however, can often indulge travel writers with anything from 1000–2000 words.

Starting up

In theory, all you need is pen and paper but in practice you'll need more if you want to appear as professional as possible. Regrettably, an article typed on a portable typewriter no longer gives the right image.

A word processor (See Chapter 12) will save you an enormous amount of time rewriting and resubmitting articles, but remember that you have to invest a considerable amount of time at the outset in mastering it and becoming familiar with its little idiosyncrasies. More than once I've pressed the wrong button and lost an entire morning's work, but persevere and eventually the day will come when you couldn't live without it.

It pays to have some business cards printed, and letterheads too. Once you have a fair amount of manuscripts out on spec, an answering machine is a good investment. However much people affect to detest them, they are extremely useful, for editors are frequently too busy to write, are short of time and prefer to phone with last minute queries, requests for photographs, or even – yes, it does happen – wondering if you have any ideas to fill their columns. If you have an answering machine they can leave a message: if they can't reach you they will move on to another contributor to whom they can get through.

Tax deductible expenses

Keep invoices not only for the large and more expensive items you purchase such as answering machines, fax machines and word processors, but for all the stationery you buy too; the notebooks, biros, envelopes, business cards, paper, staples, Scotch tape, disks and typewriter ribbons, as these are legitimate expenses which are allowable against income tax.

Obviously you can't claim expenses against income tax for writing travel articles unless you have some income from writing to show for it. The expenses you claim must be wholly and exclusively incurred in writing, although not necessarily travel writing, and include:

Travel expenses
Hotel expenses
Telephone, postage, photocopying and typing
A certain proportion of the costs of using your home as office
Professional research
Professional journals
Photographic equipment

Word processors, fax and answering machines and the more expensive items of photographic equipment are considered to be capital items and qualify for a 25% writing down allowance.

If you work from home you can claim a proportion of the running costs of your house (including electricity, gas and even mortgage interest) in proportion to the number of rooms you have – if you use one room in a four room house for writing, then you will normally get tax relief on one fourth of the total.

Beware of capital gains tax liability, however, if you designate one room exclusively as an office and subsequently sell your house. Tax experts advise using the spare bedroom or even the kitchen as your 'office' rather than a designated room. It can still be claimed for expenses without the danger of incurring a capital gains charge.

Keep records of everything you spend in the course of your writing, and of all the cheques which you receive in payment. It is also a good idea to keep your rejection slips as proof that you are actively engaged in writing, even if you are not getting the rewards you feel you deserve. A sympathetic tax inspector will realise that the expenses involved in writing a guide book, for instance, frequently exceed the publisher's advance and that you have to supplement this by submitting articles to other markets. Even if these submissions do not invariably result in cheques, at least the rejection slips are evidence that you have been working.

Keep your copy clean

Whether you work at a portable, an electronic typewriter or a word processor, the manuscript should be double spaced on A4 paper with wide margins and corrections kept to the absolute minimum – if you have more than two or three to a page, retype the page. This is no problem on a word processor, but on a typewriter can take more time than you can spare. Typing the correction on a self-adhesive label and stripping it in over the mistake looks far neater and more unobtrusive than numerous corrections in ink, and is quicker than retyping. Obviously you don't want your manuscript to look as if it has been in the wars, so use this solution with discretion.

Research the market

There are over 10,000 publications in the UK ranging from Sunday papers to local freebies, glossy magazines like *Vogue* and *Harper's* to those grouped as trade, technical and professional. Add in courtesy magazines, annuals and house journals and it means that there are a great many opportunities waiting to be exploited by the energetic tiro travel writer. It isn't easy, but the important thing is to persevere. Subscribe to publications such as *Freelance Market News*, *Writers' Monthly* and *Writers News* which give detailed information on new and existing markets, editorial requirements and whether to submit ideas or the completed manuscript.

Your market study should also include the *Writers' & Artists' Yearbook* and *The Writer's Handbook*, both of which give details of hundreds of publications which are potential buyers of freelance material, their editorial requirements and payment. Additionally, they are excellent sources of inspiration when, off-hand, you cannot think of any publication likely to be interested in your rather esoteric trip through the jungles of New Guinea. Neither of these annuals covers the entire spectrum of publications, however, and *Benn's Media*, normally available in the reference section of most public libraries, is a useful supplement as it gives the names and addresses of most publications in the UK. It doesn't, however, give either editorial requirements or details of payment.

Market research helps you find markets that you might not normally come across but it is necessary to study the actual publications themselves to find the house style – is it formal or chatty, do they publish first-person travel articles or do they favour factual and impersonal ones? Do they prefer famous names, not necessarily from the travel world, for – to the chagrin of professional travel writers – television personalities, novelists, actors and actresses, footballers and rock stars are frequently sent on agreeable assignments to write about Italy, Australia, China and India for everything from the *TV Times* to the tabloids.

Expand your horizons

Unless you already have a great store of travel experience through your work, it is always a good idea to expand your travel horizons as much as possible by going to the special promotional evenings which travel agents hold periodically – usually in a local hotel – in many towns throughout Britain. The format is to show a video or slides devoted to a theme which they are promoting, be it cruising, skiing, California or Florida, supplemented by a question and answer session and suitable refreshments. The idea, naturally, is to create interest and, if possible, to convert that interest into a booking, to sell you a holiday to the USA or tempt you to a cruise on the QE2, but there is absolutely nothing to stop you going to one of these special evenings in search of ideas.

Tour operators' brochures are themselves good sources of ideas, especially the ones which include 'editorial' on their destinations. Brittany Ferries' Gîte Holidays brochure, for instance, not only has beguiling descriptions of each of the regions of France in which they have gîtes – simple but comfortable converted French farm buildings and cottages – but is also enlightening about the foods and attractions of each region.

Generally speaking, the more up-market and expensive the holiday, the more expensive and expansive the brochure, which will woo with words and seductive photographs. Tour operators whose particular patch is the mass-market concentrate more on prices, hotel details, flights and children's discounts than the scenery. So a visit to your travel agent is seldom wasted, and may indeed be quite productive – in fact I've probably picked up more leads from reading travel brochures than guide books.

Most of the national tourist offices are situated in London, and if you get the opportunity to visit them you will be able to browse through all the brochures they have on display in search of ideas. You can also get information by post, but in this case you will have to be more specific and request a brochure or leaflet on a certain town or region. You can also phone for information, but as the telephone lines of many tourist offices seem perpetually engaged it may take days to get through to them. Increasingly, too, offices are employing 0891 telephone numbers. This means that you, the caller, are paying for the call at an expensive rate and have no control over the length of time it will take to get the information you need.

Clip the coupons in the national press for brochures you may need such as the English Tourist Board's annual publication, *Let's Go*, which details two-day breaks throughout England and gives thumbnail sketches of each region.

Sources of ideas

There are Tourist Information Centres in towns of any size throughout Britain and, although some of them are notably more helpful than others, the best ones provide a pick-up point for information on travel-related topics not only in the town itself but in the wider area around. Hotel brochures, restaurants, stately homes, National Trust properties, recreational facilities, boat trips, coach tours, gardens open to the public, historic pubs, town walks, zoos, celebrated figures in the town's past and museums – there are leaflets galore vying for attention on the notice boards and shelves of the tourist office. But best of all, from the writer's point of view, you will find details of local themes and trails there.

On a national basis in the UK throughout the past few years, there have been promotions tied to a specific theme – Victorian Scotland, Norman Britain, the Gardens of England, Maritime England, Britain's Spa Heritage, etc. – which have been tremendously successful in attracting overseas visitors to Britain. They have also been successful in encouraging the British themselves to be more adventurous in exploring other parts of their own island, pointing them in the direction of the best Norman abbeys, the finest Victorian buildings, the most unusual gardens.

The object of these themes has been to get overseas visitors away from the capital to parts of the country which are well worth seeing but largely unknown to the thousands of French, Germans, Americans and Japanese who visit our shores each year – rewarding cities like St Albans, for instance, and gardens such as Inverewe in the Scottish Highlands.

On a smaller scale, each region has caught on to the value of local 'trails'. How they exploit this notion may vary – some tourist offices recommend suitable hotels en route, others ignore the commercial aspect – but this kind of promotion is a gift to the travel writer, as it provides a constantly enlarging source of interesting material. And travel editors who don't have time to investigate personally may be ready to commission or accept articles from freelance travel writers on these themes.

Scotland, naturally, has its Robert Burns Trail and its ever popular Whisky Trails. The West Country is particularly enterprising, publishing no less than three heritage trails: King Arthur Country, which guides visitors to places associated with this great legendary figure; Lorna Doone Country which concentrates on the Exmoor of R.D. Blackmore's famous novel and Thomas Hardy's Wessex which takes visitors through places in Dorset such as Dorchester, Sherborne, Puddletown and Bere Regis – the Casterbridge, Sherton Abbas, Weatherbury and Kingsbere of his *Mayor of Casterbridge*, *Far from the Madding Crowd* and *Tess of the D'Urbervilles* novels.

Whitby has gone in for a Dracula Trail – visitors can follow in the footsteps of the fearsome count, the product of Bram Stoker's vivid imagination as he sat on a seat overlooking Whitby harbour. Tyneside is exploiting its Catherine Cookson connection with visits to places which form the setting or are mentioned in her best-selling novels. The National Trust also publishes booklets on a different theme each year – sometimes even as many as three or four in a particularly eventful year.

Hotels often give a great deal of useful information in their brochures about the tourist attractions in the surrounding area such as golf courses, stately homes and their approximate distances from the hotel, while the bigger hotel groups frequently publish their own local trail or theme leaflets. Although the material naturally covers their own hotels and excludes what may well be the equally relevant material of their rivals across the street, their leaflets often suggest ideas and save a great deal of research.

Heritage trails, of course, aren't just the prerogative of the British. France has them too, with Richard the Lion Heart and even Robert Louis Stevenson themes. The secret is to discover one which matches the interests of the market you are aiming at.

If you are still stuck for ideas, trawl around the leaflets available in your local library for details of local walks, stately homes, nature reserves, and interesting historical associations to add to your ideas resource file. Better still, a visit to an unfamiliar library – even one only a dozen miles away – will often give a jump-start to your ideas when local libraries fail.

Think ahead for opportunities

Keep a diary of notable anniversaries coming up next year; you may have the qualifications to write an article on a particular country, and a forthcoming anniversary provides an excellent opportunity to remind editors about it and suggest an article.

The announcement of a forthcoming visit by one of the Royals or the Prime Minister to a country you know well is the moment to start preparing your query letter or the completed article. Particularly in the case of the Queen's State visits, the announcements are made well ahead of the actual date, giving you plenty of time to write an article. Send it to the first newspaper of your choice at least a month before the visit, with a covering letter to remind the travel editor of the dates the V.I.P.s will be in the country. But as magazines work much further ahead – usually 8–12 weeks in the case of the glossies – it is none too early to send your article in at least four months ahead of the planned visit.

Never send the same article to more than one publication at a time: if you do, and the article appears in both, you have had it as a travel writer. Unfortunately, with submissions keyed to specific dates, if the first publication you send it to doesn't bother to return your manuscript promptly – as, regrettably, happens quite regularly – it is likely to be too late to send it out again and the opportunity is lost for good.

A phone call may establish whether or not the editor is interested in principle, but even this doesn't guarantee publication, however well the article is written, for the demands of advertising at a particular moment may mean the editorial pages have to be cut and your article axed. Most articles can still be used in the coming months but topical articles which have passed their 'sell-by' date obviously have no future.

On the other hand, you may be lucky. My own entrée to the nationals came through an article on Bermuda which I sent in on spec after the announcement of a forthcoming political Summit meeting on the island, and whereas I anticipated its publication would be timed to coincide with the Summit it appeared a week or two before, just as a group of invited travel writers was returning from a 'familiarisation' trip to Bermuda – all set, in fact, to dash to their word processors while the subject matter was highly topical.

4
Write From Experience

Much as I dislike the advice invariably given to aspiring writers, 'Write about what you know', (heaven help novelists or sci-fi writers), I have to admit that it holds true for would-be travel writers. It may be a memorable visit to Sydney, to Tenby or to Nashville or – as in the case of a correspondent who wrote to me recently – a year spent living on a houseboat on the Bosphurus which leads you into travel writing rather than transmuting your experiences into fiction or poetry, but it's obvious that what you saw, felt and heard is the raw material of your article or book.

Create your own opportunities

Although it may have been some exotic travel experiences that gave you the impetus to submit your first travel article, you don't have to wait for another exotic trip before you write your next article. Many people whose travel is constrained by lack of money, young children, fear of flying or a dozen other perfectly legitimate reasons feel they have nothing to contribute to the total sum of travel writing. 'My experiences are too mundane,' a cyclist friend just back from Ireland told me. 'Editors are only interested in glamorous destinations.' Wrong. What editors are interested in is covered in Chapter 2, and it's not by any means limited to glamorous destinations. Here are thirteen ideas to keep you writing:

Travelling with children

Young mothers often feel they are at a disadvantage when it comes to travel writing; that a trip to Sainsbury's in the nearest town with a couple of toddlers is all the travel and adventure that they are likely to achieve until the children are older. But even if you can't afford to visit Disney World, remember that the majority of parents in this country are in the same boat, and that Britain, too, has its theme parks, and a visit to Alton Towers may be an achievable goal. What were you expecting? How did the children react? Which of the several restaurants did you eat in? Which of the themed areas did the children enjoy most? What souvenirs did you buy? Did you/the children/grandparents find it tiring/exhausting/expensive/value for money?

If, as a young mother, you are really determined to be a travel writer, then what is needed is the will to get into print and an ability to create your own opportunities. The former travel editor of the *Daily Telegraph*, Elisabeth de Stroumillo, went to enormous trouble to make travel possible:

> In my early travel-writing days, needing to be mobile for the job, to have my children with me for pleasure, and to watch every penny I spent, my long-suffering spouse and I 'created' our own motor-caravans from secondhand vehicles bought very cheaply: a two-ton delivery truck (basic and uncomfortable), a mobile shop (comfortable but achingly slow), and an ambulance (best of all, well-sprung and reasonably nippy). All these experiences were on the whole a success, satisfying my own gipsy instincts and the children's need for amusement combined with a modicum of security.

In its range of possibilities, travel with babies and young children is limited only by the imagination and Susan Grossman's book *Have Children, Will Travel*, shows the market is by no means limited to magazine and newspaper articles. Children's holiday discounts, adventure camps for children, your experience of flying to the States with a six week old baby and a seven year old (how did the airline cope, did they provide nappies, warm the baby's bottle, provide games to occupy the older child on this long-haul trip, would they have provided 'aunties' to escort your elder child if he had been flying alone? How did you cope with changing the baby's nappies on a crowded plane?).

Holidays under canvas have clubs to keep children occupied, provide books to help them identify flowers and animals, and offer prizes for writing and painting competitions. Most cross-channel ferries provide playrooms for younger children and quizzes to keep the older ones occupied during the journey. Shipping companies and tour operators run short – and inexpensive – trips abroad to that popular attraction for children, Legoland, near Esbjerg in Denmark. Contrary to what you might assume, having children doesn't limit you as far as travel writing is concerned. Instead they will provide you with a ready fund of travel material. Don't, however, make the mistake of thinking that because you are writing about children that your market is restricted to magazines such as *Mother & Baby, Baby, Parents* etc. Explore the possibilities of nationals such as *Good Housekeeping*, caravanning and motoring magazines, and the scope provided by newspapers.

Travelling on foot and by caravan

Walking may not sound as glamorous as jetting all over the world, but it can lead to contributing articles about walks in your own country and, given the will and the opportunity, lead to travel and adventure in most parts of the world, as witness Eric Newby and his *Short Walk in the Hindu Kush*. The late Alfred Wainwright's name was synonymous with fell-walking in the Lake District and he wrote over sixty books about his walks, all best-sellers in their sphere.

Walking knows no social barriers; travel articles with walks as the theme appear in everything from *The Climber* to the Sundays and nationals such as the *Daily Telegraph*, (although their articles come from a regular contributor.)

Country Walking, a magazine launched as a bi-monthly, recently went monthly. 'The response has been phenomenal and clearly indicates this is a market with a lot of potential,' said the publisher.

Great Outdoors, a magazine which deals with walking, backpacking and countryside topics, welcomes unsolicited manuscripts but its standards are high, and it is not enough just to put one's itinerary down baldly on paper. The following extract from an article about walking through the Peak District conveys the feel of the countryside with the skill of a novelist:

> 'The rough gritstone wall that zig-zagged like the wanderings of a
> drunken sailor was warm to my back; the clump of heather on which
> I sat soft and spongy. The sun shone from a sky streaked with thin,
> silvery wisps of cottonwool cloud.'

Explore the opportunities offered by magazines such as *Camping* or *Climber & Hill Walking* which has articles on mountaineering and hill-walking in the UK and abroad.

Independent travellers who have just walked through the Borneo jungle or some similar long-haul and off-beat destination could, with sufficient photographs of first-class quality, find a market in *The Traveller*, a glossy magazine published by Wexas, a tour operator specialising in long-haul journeys for independent travellers.

Thousands of people have experience of caravanning and there are many magazines devoted to their interests, most of them containing articles on travel at home and abroad with a caravan: *Practical Caravan*, for example, currently contains articles on 'Heading South to the Med.' and 'Guide to 50 Farm Trails', while

Caravan Magazine looks for 'real life experiences of touring by caravan, especially if well-illustrated by photographs'. Both *Motor Caravan Magazine* and *Motorcaravan and Motorhome Monthly* carry touring features at home and abroad.

The business traveller

Top businessmen, especially those who travel on expense accounts, inhabit a world of international airports, de luxe hotels, fashionable restaurants, car-hire and credit cards. If this is your milieu, then it is very likely that your experiences will enable you to contribute to the magazines which cater for the business traveller. There are two dominating the UK market: *Business Traveller*, which has a controlled circulation, and *E.T.* (the new name of *Executive Travel*), a monthly magazine for business travellers. Although both cater for roughly the same market, they have a different approach. The former is concerned with value-for-money travel, the most economical ways of getting from London to Singapore, for example, and has a large number of pages devoted to readers' letters, sharing their travel experiences with other equally peripatetic businessmen. *E.T.* on the other hand is dominated by destination pieces.

Nearly every airline publishes its own magazine, and since businessmen travelling Club class, or the foreign equivalent, are their bread, butter, and quite often the caviar, too, the magazine is not infrequently dominated by travel articles. *High Life*, British Airways in-flight magazine, invariably has several, while others carry travel articles on places pertinent to their main routes. There can't be many people whose choice of airline is influenced by the in-flight magazine, but for travel writers on the look-out for new markets, the idea is not too far out.

A 2000 word article on Norway in Air UK's magazine *Bluebird* (a forerunner of its present title, *Flagship*), sparked off the idea for what has now become a major tourist attraction. The writer explored the Rogoland region between Stavanger and the historic Hanseatic city of Bergen by using ferries and his article on the unexploited possibilities attracted the attention of a tour operator, who promptly launched a 'Fjord Hopper' tour. Awarding the writer of the article the title of 'Honorary Tourist Consul', Norway's director of tourism in London claimed, 'The most exciting aspect is that this tour came from the creative mind of a writer.'

Hotel groups of the type frequented by businessmen usually publish a glossy magazine on a quarterly or twice-yearly basis. This is seldom produced in-house; quite a few publishing companies exist solely to edit and publish these 'courtesy' magazines on the hotel's behalf. Here the travel article concentration is most likely to be on the area in the immediate vicinity of the hotel, and may well be aimed at overseas guests. Hotel magazines are not an easy target market for travel articles unless you are familiar both with the hotels themselves, and the magazine. That said, most of the big hotel groups such as Forte and Holiday Inns publish magazines for the benefit of their guests.

If business takes you jetting around the world to conferences and those international exhibitions which seem to spin round Europe and the States at a hectic pace, then you will be familiar with the inside of more conference rooms, conference suites and conference halls than you care to remember. But conference suites do not exist in limbo. They lend themselves to destination pieces. Is the conference centre in the city centre? Can you reach it by public transport if it is situated at the very edge of the city? What is the atmosphere like – ultra-modern and hightech with all the latest audio-visual gadgets laid on and instantaneous translation? Or a former church converted to a conference hall, with few amenities beyond a microphone, but strong in history and prestige? Are city tours laid on for the wives of conference delegates? Again, a travel article, aimed at a specialised market rather than the tourist, but travel writing nevertheless. Magazines in this market include *Conferences & Exhibitions*, *Incentive Travel*, and *Delegates*. Not that this type of market is exclusively confined to these specialised publications. Even *The Sunday Times* travel section carried an article on unusual conference venues, which included the London Zoo, the chartering of an InterCity train, the Palace of Versailles and the thirteenth-century prison on the Ile de la Cité in Paris.

Travelling in retirement

Being retired is no bar to travel writing and may indeed be a positive advantage, for it not only gives you leisure and opportunities for travel that you may never have enjoyed before but also an insider's view of an increasingly significant market.

There are over ten million people in the UK over the age of 60, a sizable market which offers considerable potential to tour operators. The more tempting the offers, the more alluring the destinations, the bigger their share of the market; naturally tour operators spend considerable money on advertising and producing seductive-looking brochures. However, next to word-of-mouth recommendations, reading about a particular resort or destination, or seeing it on ITV's *Wish You Were Here* or the BBC's *Holiday* programme, is a much more influential way of getting people to choose the particular holidays which are on offer to the public.

Saga have long been the leaders in holidays for older people and publish a popular magazine ten times a year. Although the articles are by no means all on travel *per se*, many are on what might well be described as 'travel-related' subjects – human interest with a travel background.

With the trend towards earlier retirement, magazines for this market are correspondingly lowering their target age group. *Active Life, Yours, 050* and *Choice* cater for the over-fifty-fives, with an emphasis on travel, although it must be admitted that these are frequently staff written.

As well as writing magazine and newspaper articles on travel in retirement there is mileage in books on the subject. One of the dozen books written by Dan Lees, a former *Daily Express* staff reporter, and his wife Molly, is *Travel in Retirement*. To quote the blurb: 'Packed with money-saving, worry-saving ideas on where to go and how to get there. How to get the best possible deal from airlines, shipping lines, resorts and hotels. Chapters cover the delights of motoring, walking and cycling in retirement (a quarter of the Cyclists' Touring Club are over 50), and suggests ways to spend winters in the sun at a cheaper cost than staying at home.'

Transport

Transport is a specialised branch of travel writing where the opportunities of first-hand experience are many. Elizabeth Gundrey's books on touring *England by Bus* have been instant successes and should inspire those who feel they can't write on travel because they lack the opportunity to travel abroad. Her books, full of ideas for exploring the prettier parts of England, include details of stately homes, National Trust properties and historic cities easily reached by bus and coach.

Articles on using the local bus service to explore Brittany and Normandy have appeared in *The Observer*, and features on travelling from New York to San Francisco or Chicago to New Orleans by Greyhound bus appear with great regularity in student publications and not infrequently in the Sundays too.

When it comes to car travel, don't overlook the opportunities presented by the glossy magazines published by Toyota, Honda, Mercedes and many more car manufacturers.

But of all forms of transport, trains, particularly steam trains, are possibly the most popular, certainly with men, and it is a rewarding subject in which to specialise. Sampling famous trains with all their creature comforts such as South Africa's Blue Train from Cape Town to Johannesburg, Japan's Bullet trains, and the E & O, the Eastern and Oriental Express which links Singapore, Kuala Lumpur and Bangkok in air-conditioned comfort, means that you are seldom at a loss for something to write about, and the excitement of unexpectedly coming across an ancient steam train in China or Peru need not be confined to the pages of *Railway World*.

Nearer home, the little railways of Wales, the Bluebell Line, or the famous Watercress Line which diligently puffs its way through the Hampshire countryside from Alton to Alresford not only provide material for travel articles but might become subjects for the 'Day Out' articles which are increasingly in demand for the expanded leisure sections of the nationals at weekends.

Next to railways, canals and inland waterways will provide you with never-ending themes to write about, not just for magazines such as *Canal and Riverboat*, but for guide books, overseas publications in search of new angles on the tourist theme, and, of course, the nationals, most of whose travel features regularly major on the delights of leisurely travelling through France by canal, cycling to the nearest village to buy fruit, practising one's French on the lock-keepers, and eating like gastronomes in wayside bistros for less than the price of a cup of coffee and a gâteau in Great Britain.

Specialising in food

Food is a subject which merges smoothly into travel articles. Most people enjoy reading about food; about shopping for fresh asparagus and ripe apricots in markets, and searching out specialist shops from which they can carry exotic ingredients or *bain maries* home in triumph like a trophy. Have you ever read a travel article on Boulogne which doesn't mention Philippe Olivier's marvellous cheese shop on the Rue Thiers, for instance? Not infrequently food takes over to such an extent that it dominates the article. Entire articles can (and have) been written on what food loot to bring back from a day trip to France, let alone a fortnight's. Travel with a theme of food running through it is a formula which is popular with upmarket magazines generally, and airline and credit card company magazines in particular.

For the travel writer interested in food, there is every opportunity nowadays to exploit this current interest. To mix a metaphor or two, it is a deep well to draw on – from strange foods like the crocodile burgers which can now be found on Australian menus to restaurants abroad run by Britons. One of the most successful combinations of travel and food that has come my way was an article devoted to a Belgian town whose main distinction was no fewer than six restaurants with one or more Michelin stars. It appeared in an airline magazine and no doubt other travel writers are currently scouring the pages of the red Michelin guides in search of similar inspiration.

Courtesy magazines – the name given to those magazines provided free for guests, customers or passengers by hotels, car hire firms and airlines – published in the UK are equally interested in food/travel writing. Since a sizable proportion of their guests at any one time are from overseas, articles on regional food and dishes such as Stargazzy Pie, Arbroath Smokies, Manx kippers, Edinburgh Rock, and where to find them/buy them/enjoy them are of consuming interest. And not only the dishes themselves, but where they may be eaten, too, is of consequence. Picnics, fish and chips, and pub grub probably interest just as many foreigners as do five star restaurants, although the market you are aiming at when writing a food article will inevitably dictate the content.

The traditional dishes of our multi-ethnic society are growing so popular that they have become a tourist attraction in their own right. Visitors come from abroad to enjoy Bradford's curry tours and Birmingham is rapidly becoming famous for its Balti dishes.

Wines tend to be the province of Masters of Wine or the wine correspondents who concentrate on this subject for the nationals. But they write about it first and foremost from the wine taster's angle, the soil, the vines, the micro-climate and the grape varieties, their nose, colour, tannin and acidity. This leaves the travel writer to pursue wine trails through Alsace, concentrating on the scenery and suitable places to taste the wines. You could also write on subjects such as courses on wine-appreciation in Champagne country which fall naturally into the 'weekend breaks' or 'learning breaks' type of article.

Nearer home, there are a steadily increasing number of vineyards throughout England, particularly throughout the south of England, and descriptions of these can be geared to the tourist market. CAMRA (Campaign for Real Ale) has alerted the public to the possibilities of beer and ale from independent brewers up and down the country – a subject in which many travel writers would relish specialising.

Plenty of travel books have evolved from the pursuit of food and wine. Patricia Fenn's series *French Entrée* and Arthur Eperon's *Traveller's France* both major on food and wine, hotels and restaurants, and there are dozens of local guides throughout Britain sharing the same preoccupations.

The self-catering market

Self-catering holidays are popular and, increasingly, readers are anxious to know the rewards and snags. It is perfectly possible to rent a luxury villa in Mustique but most people's idea of a self-catering holiday is more modest, a cottage deep in Somerset, perhaps, preferably thatched, a gîte in the Dordogne, an apartment in Rimini. Apart from articles, books such as Susan Grossman's *Self-Catering in Italy* and Bill Glenton's *Self-Catering Afloat* show how the subject can be developed beyond the predictable.

Inevitably, as frequently happens, as soon as you start researching, other avenues open up, giving you the opportunity to expand the subject matter beyond anything you had first envisaged: properties such as the seaside cottages and apartments in Scottish castles which can be rented from the National Trust, for instance, and the curious and interesting buildings available for rent from the Landmark Trust.

With the down turn in farming, farmers and their families are now looking for other ways of making money, not least by 'people farming' – offering holidays down on the farm. Each farm is different: some transform their redundant cottages into simple self-catering units with never an animal in sight, some provide hearty bed and breakfast to overnight guests, others provide cordon bleu meals and en suite bathrooms inside and plenty of animals outside to remind you that you are actually staying on a farm.

Wedding bells

It's probably easier to fly away and get married in Barbados or some equally relaxed part of the world nowadays than it is to stay at home and get married in your local church. Virgin Holidays and many other travel companies offer a complete wedding package – flowers, clergyman, champagne, certificate *et al*. All you have to do is decide whether to get married by the pool or on the beach. Unfortunately, however, so many couples have married abroad by now that the subject has little novelty value as far as publications catering for brides and weddings are concerned. Which is not to say that there isn't a market somewhere if you think laterally.

Being the mother of a bride who was getting married in Ceylon, for instance, gave one writer the chance to write a travel article on Ceylon – the bride was merely the hook. And at Cromlix House, a country house hotel with its own chapel in Perthshire, Scotland, they have been hosting weddings for years – but not all the weddings are for Scots. A good number of their weddings are arranged (by fax) for Americans, who regard a trip to Scotland and a marriage ceremony complete with piper in attendance as deeply romantic. The first article appeared in a magazine for the over-50s market, the second in an overseas publication.

The Westin hotel in Tokyo has both a traditional Shinto wedding hall and a western-style wedding chapel within the property and although few Japanese are Christians, the Christian wedding service is the one 90% of the couples ask for. In Las Vegas they have wedding chapels with coy names like Wee Kirk o' the Heather and the Hitching Post, while one of Joan Collins' many marriage ceremonies took place at the Little White Chapel. So if you're lucky enough to get an invitation to a wedding when you're abroad, don't turn it down. Even when you're not directly involved, it's another experience to write about.

Activity holidays

The current interest in activity holidays, from bird watching in Spain to sub-aqua in the Red Sea, correspondingly widens travel writing opportunities. The market for riding articles, in particular, extends beyond magazines such as *Horse and Riding* (which takes articles on riding with a travel background) to the general domain of the nationals. An interest in horses can also provide the starting point for travel articles. Pompadour in France calls itself 'The City of the Horse' and can be compared with Newmarket; staying on a dude ranch in the USA is a popular subject, particularly with magazines catering for the under-30s. The wild horses of the Camargue, the wild ponies of the New Forest, the racecourses of Australia, the horse and camel races in Bahrain, are all legitimate travel subjects suggested by riding and horses.

Nowadays many people are rejecting the idea of lying on a beach all day, preferring to use their holidays learning to paint or fly, go surfing, climbing or canoeing. Imagine the plight of the staff writer, suddenly assigned to go on an activity holiday about which he is not particularly enthused: rather than write the assignment himself, the chances are he will want to pass the invitation on to someone able to write intelligently about the subject.

Not that beach holidays as a form of specialisation are to be despised – plenty of people still crave nothing more than two weeks stretched out in the sand, the hotter the better. Parents of young families are constantly in need of updating about beaches – safe ones for the toddlers, ones with some action nearby in the evening so that the teenagers won't get bored. Some readers are keen to know of beaches where they can go topless without offending local mores, others where they can go skinny dipping without being arrested. How clean are the beaches? In Italy, many of the beaches are private; how much might it add to the cost of a holiday there if you lie on the beach all day?

Similar to activity holidays are those which offer to teach new skills, such as computing (even the Q.E.II offers a computer room, with tuition, as you cross the Atlantic), or studying a subject in which you are interested. During the long vacations, universities and many public schools open their doors to 'Summer Academies', where you can study subjects as diverse as 'The Rise of Devon Seaside Resorts', 'Victorian Fiction', 'Scottish Landscape Painting' and 'Developing your Creativity'.

The religious market

In spite of the steadily increasing number of tours organised to shrines and places of Biblical significance by church groups, and the number of Bishops and other clergy who travel on Swan Hellenic Tours as lecturers, the religious press is a largely unexplored seam of specialised interest. The *Jewish Chronicle*, the *Catholic Herald* and *The Universe* all carry regular travel articles. Although these are by no means angled exclusively round destinations with religious connections, a travel article written from first-hand experience about a religious festival abroad, a place of pilgrimage, or historical connection with a biblical figure would have the edge over a general travel article.

Conservation and heritage

Conservation is one of the 'in' topics of the moment, and one that has more relevance to tourism than most. As nature reserves give way to airport runways, palm trees are axed to make way for skyscraper hotels, and the Greek Islands are overrun by camera-carrying tourists, so the debate hots up. Nowadays almost anything of value, whether environmental, historical or archaeological which has been saved from the developer fires the attention of travel writers, whereas a decade or so ago such concerns might have passed unnoticed. Magazines such as *Country Life*, *The Field* and *Shooting* prefer their travel articles to look at conservation themes rather than describe hedonistic pleasures.

The restoration of waterfront developments such as Bristol, Swansea and Liverpool and of the dilapidated dock areas of London and their transformation into vibrant centres of activity with craft shops, boats, yacht basins, cafes and boutiques, has its parallels in cities such as Boston and Baltimore in the USA and throughout Europe.

Green tourism

Not so long ago, no one had even heard of green tourism. Nowadays, of course, the subject is regularly aired in the media and everyone is becoming increasing conscious of the need to consider our environment. Nature has become a marketable asset, and several tour companies have evolved which concentrate on keeping tourism and tourists in harmony with the local communities they visit, for unrestrained tourism harms not just the environment – it can cause great social and economic damage too. Tourists often put a great strain on the water-supply in third world countries, for instance, and while luxury hotels may employ local people, their profits are often remitted back overseas.

If you have experience of travelling with a company which believes in travelling sensitively, in living with the local community in India or Africa and using locally-owned transport and hotels rather than international ones, or if you are early on the scene of one of the new green programmes being initiated by tourist offices throughout Europe, then you are well placed to suggest articles to a wide range of publications, from the nationals to airline magazines.

But don't try to proselytise about the subject in your travel articles. Remember it's the story of your trip, what you saw, what you did, and who you met that interests and influences readers most. And don't lose sight of the fact that green tourism is not solely a concern for our environment but a term used to market everything from cycling holidays in the UK, bird watching in Dubai, whale watching in California and swimming with dolphins off the Azores.

Hobbies and collections

Don't overlook the mileage from writing about travel-related hobbies such as collecting guide books, postcards, stamps, watercolours of foreign ports, etc. – subjects in which you are already interested and about which you may know a great deal. Postcards in particular have great potential, but to interest a wider audience try to find an angle beyond the postcard itself, like the American who came across 50 sepia-tinted postcards of Indonesia dating from the 1920s in a junk shop in Connecticut. He took them with him on a visit to Indonesia, showed them to his guide and was amazed when she identified one of the views on the card as her grand-mother's home. They visited her and heard stories of the other scenes, some of which had disappeared in the intervening years. Appropriately titled 'Life in the Old Card Yet' and illustrated by some of the well-travelled postcards, the article had human as well as collector's interest and was published in the in-flight magazine of Garuda, Indonesia's national airline.

5
'I Wish I'd Said That': The creative part

To be able to recreate the smells, the sounds, the tastes and colours of a country so vividly that it jumps to life off the printed page, to capture the essence and character of a place in a few phrases, is the aim of every travel writer. To be able to share your experiences on a remote Scottish island, on safari in Kenya or sightseeing in Shanghai so evocatively that your readers immediately make it their ambition to see the country for themselves is the ultimate accolade.

It is a talent which comes naturally to some people. Anne Gregg has it. Writing about the pleasures of France, she captures the daily ritual of life in a small French village in under 100 words:

'The village itself – the one with the croissants au beurre – has a sense of timelessness, of community, each day reawakening as shop-front blinds roll up and shutters are flung back. Pots of geraniums are being watered on steps and window sills. A man in bleu-de-travail takes Le Monde with his coffee at the cafe bar while the barman puts up Pernod parasols outside. Ancient bells echo from the tiny Romanesque church. Someone is calling 'Minou! Minou!' as a dusty kitten lurks under the parked yellow La Poste van.'

Fortunately for the rest of us there are ways of keeping subject matter alive and vivid which can be learned. Travel writing is all about painting pictures in words as in *Brazilian Adventure*, Peter Fleming's book, when, back in Europe, he reflected on

'the small diurnal things which various stages of our journey had stamped many times upon my mind. The hot sand squeaking as we plodded through it: the plaintive whiffling of the little otters . . . the familiar play of muscles in the paddlers' backs . . . the taste of too many bananas.'

Banal travel articles undoubtedly do get into print, usually by a combination of fluke circumstances, such as the last minute withdrawal of an advertisement and the article in question being exactly the right length to fill the gap. But although having one article accepted by a publication often ensures a friendly reception for further suggestions, the author of a travel article empty of interesting facts and local colour is unlikely to get a second chance.

Observe with all your senses

Travel writing starts long before you can put a single word of description down on paper. First comes observation, looking around you not just at the scenery but at your fellow travellers – how they are dressed, how they behave. It is amazing how many people are on automatic pilot, travelling between work and home each day more or less oblivious to their surroundings, incurious and uninterested. The best journalists are invariably the most observant. If you are not observant by nature then you can develop this ability by practising every day on your fellow travellers on the bus or tube – people you meet casually are easier to start with than people you are close to. Observe their clothes, the way they wear them, their attitudes (body language, if you like). Are they fidgety, do they look happy, sad, depressed, confident, do they carry their belongings in plastic bags or briefcases? Do these give clues to the type of work they do?

It is not enough to observe only with your eyes. Use your nose and ears too. A lively description of the sounds and smells of a country is as important to an article or book as describing that the most important building in the capital had a pink colour wash, as this review of a book about Paris demonstrates:

> 'A wonderful evocation of café life between the wars with its distinctive odour: a mixture of cigarette smoke, garlic, hot chocolate, cognac and water, and the Guerlain perfume called 'L'Heure Bleue.'

Don't talk about sounds and smells in general – describe them. What kind of smells – pleasant, unpleasant? Woodsmoke, pine trees, freshly baked bread, garlic, bad drains, body-smells? What kind of sounds? Soft, loud? Discordant, musical? Teasing, beguiling, seductive? Birdsong, the soft plash of fountains? Or are they in some way threatening? Raised voices, distant drums, yelping dogs? The following account of bringing in the New Year in Manila is much more effective than merely describing Manila as 'noisy with New Year revellers':

> 'Manila was in a party mood. Horns blasted, music blared, dogs howled. Firecrackers fizzled and spat, and burning car tyres belched smoke at the roadside. A thick black smog hung low over the city.'

And you can hear as well as see Reid's Hotel in Madeira from this description:

'your bedroom door shuts with a Rolls-Royce clunk, elephantine lavatory seats are fashioned in wood, while baths empty with mad gurgles like the *Titanic* going down'.

Conversely, it may not be noise which overwhelms you, but silence. Writing about Cairo and the Plague in 1835, Alexander Kinglake, the author of that great travel classic, *Eothen*, wrote: 'Although the plague was now spreading quick and terrible havoc around him, I did not see very plainly change in the looks of the streets until the seventh day after my arrival. I then first observed that the city was silenced.'

Give that tree a name

Bring out the details of your surroundings by naming names – in other words personalising them. Writing 'We drove down a sweeping drive lined with flamboyant trees/chestnut/gum trees' is much more vivid than if you had merely written 'We drove down a sweeping drive lined with trees'. Similarly with birds and flowers – what kind of birds and flowers fill the hotel garden, for instance? Hummingbirds and bougainvillaea/larks and meadowsweet/sea-gulls and seathrift? By identifying the trees, birds and flowers you have immediately given colour and identify to the scene.

Peter Chambers, a former Fleet Street travel editor, claims to have been carrying a copy of Fitter's *The Wild Flowers of Britain and Northern Europe* around with him for a couple of decades, 'ever since I decided that country walks are more interesting if you can sort out the green stuff a a bit'. It is, however, by no means easy to find out the name of a particular bird, tree or flower when in a foreign country. Guides may reel off facts and dates about long dead patriots and local heroes, plague you with ideologies and stun you with statistics, but ask them the name of the flower which grows so exuberantly over their hedges and they don't know, can't remember or give you the wrong name.

Frequently, of course, you will be on your own without a guide or native to advise you so it helps to make a rough sketch or jot down a quick description so that you can do some detective work when you return home. Leaflets and booklets from the local tourist office are often helpful, but the more exotic the country the less likely there is to be a local tourist office. Some countries, however, such as South Africa, are outstanding at providing illustrated guides to their distinctive flora and fauna.

Avoiding travel clichés

Like every other form of writing, travel writing has its clichés. In fact, as a short sortie through most travel brochures will reveal, it is a genre open to more clichés than most – a crowded strip of golden sand, blue skies and blue seas sums up dozens of sunny holiday resorts and trying to think up original alternatives on a theme of golden and blue can be an exercise leading only to sunstroke. Faced with this situation it is probably more helpful to concentrate on estimating the number of bodies to the square foot, but even here the truly creative writer shuns clichés and can describe the scene expressively and with originality. Two of my favourite quotes on overcrowded resorts are:

'There was scarcely room to squeeze a credit card between one German tourist and another.'

'The whole area has been developed to the point that only those with pollution-proof skins would risk themselves in the once healthy ocean.'

But endless descriptions of scenery, the sweet scent of frangipani and the gentle soughing of the waves on the shore are not of themselves enough to make a travel article compelling: other ingredients are needed, not least human interest. Encounters with the locals, be they former headhunters from Papua or toothless old men chewing tobacco by the side of the road in Limerick, add interest and colour. Not infrequently they may lead to an amusing and even memorable quote.

It is useless to sit in one's hotel room or relax by the hotel pool sipping piña coladas all day, under the delusion that one is absorbing local atmosphere. Holiday makers do that, travel writers go out in search of local colour, read the local papers (the small ads often give insights into what type of lives the community leads), and take themselves to places where they are most likely to encounter situations that provide good copy.

Getting orientated

The first essential for a travel writer in a foreign city is orientation. Buy a street map, not just to help you find your way around at the time but in writing the article afterwards, when you may need to describe the position of the railway station in relation to a museum or an hotel in terms of its distance from the business and shopping centre.

A visit to the tourist information centre, if there is one, is a priority. They will advise you on tours, places to visit, accommodation, restaurants, events and happenings, fêtes and festivals, theatres, home visit schemes, where to hire bikes or boats, fishing tackle or golf clubs. The books and pamphlets they carry, many of them free, are often enough to suggest subject matter for a dozen more articles.

The fastest way to orientate oneself in a strange city is to take one of the bus tours which cover the highlights of the city, the most important buildings, the main shopping street, the plazas, squares and statues which are the city's pride. Most of the tours are quite short, taking only an hour or two, and although one is seldom allowed off to see the inside of a castle or cathedral, it is a quick way of establishing priorities – which buildings are worth a return to explore in a more leisurely way, which landmarks are too far on the fringes of the city to revisit.

Explore on foot as much as possible – investigate the narrow winding streets of the old quarter, find out what lies at the top of an intriguing flight of steps, leave yourself open to the pleasures of discovering handsome buildings which no one has told you about and which are not mentioned in any travel brochure. Frequently a university campus encompasses an art gallery, an ancient theatre or historic hall – rewarding buildings which are seldom publicised but which are nonetheless open to enterprising members of the public.

Jot down street names as you walk along; they give valuable clues to a country's history and heroes. The streets and squares of South America are named after patriots and dates commemorating struggles for independence; in New Orleans they are an indication that the Spanish ruled here as well as the French; in London many prominent streets and squares are named after dukes.

Take notes

The late Nicholas Tomalin wrote that 'total recall was one of the qualities necessary to break through to the top in journalism'. Alas, few of us were born with the gift of total recall: it is easy to imagine that every little detail of a foreign trip, especially an eventful one, will stay etched in your mind for ever, but looking over old notebooks several years later will show you just how many details you have forgotten. Take notes, as full as possible in the time, either in a notebook or on tape – increasingly travellers are carrying a pocket-sized tape recorder such as a Philips notetaker (this often involves lurking in corners, apparently talking to yourself as you record

some precious detail). The choice is largely a matter of temperament. It's difficult when you have a deadline to meet to come up
with a felicitous simile, which is why it's best to note them down
immediately they occur to you. By the time you get back from
America you may have forgotten that your first reaction to the
woman you met in the bus station cafe was 'Hair like a dandelion
gone to seed', that in Scotland, 'Red deer watched us like Apache
scouts from a distant skyline' or that in Madeira the houses 'cling
to the mountainside like impending architectural avalanches.'

Even if you carry a camera it is not always possible to photograph everything you would like to. Postcards bought on the spot
are normally a good *aide mémoire.*

Mix with the locals

Serendipity plays a great part in writing about travel. You can plan
your itinerary down to the last half-hour and still end up with an
article which is perfectly competent but doesn't sparkle. Equally you
can have a totally chaotic tour, never see the beauty spots or historic
buildings you set out to visit, but still end up with a remarkably read-
able and amusing article thanks to getting lost and encountering local
characters anxious to give you directions. There are many travel trips
organised by PROs (Public Relations Officers) where you may never
meet a local at all, let alone speak to one, and in situations like this
you have to go out and make your own encounters.

Obviously if you can speak the language of the country you are
visiting you have an enormous advantage, but travel writers can't
be expected to be fluent in the language of every country they pass
through in the course of a year. Faced with Japan one week and
Russia the next, a few words of courtesy such as 'please', 'thank-
you', 'hello' and 'goodbye' are about as much as most of us can
cope with, plus the help of a good phrase book.

Bus and railway stations are good places for people-watching,
especially in Africa and South America where the passengers travel
not just with luggage but their animals too, taking a few scrawny
hens to market as well as eggs. Luggage is also revealing, particularly at airports in the Middle East. When a bomb scare at
Abu Dhabi airport made it necessary for all the luggage to be laid
out for identification on the runway, the result was a cabaret of
luggage from Gucci suitcases to clothes tied up in a bundle of black
cloth.

Souks, bazaars and street markets are a gift to travel writers for
they invariably combine human interest and local colour in an
almost unbeatable combination: pyramids of tantalising spices and

unfamiliar fruits, a mad medley of antiques, junk, plastic buckets, and clothes strange enough to start new fashion trends fascinate most people. Many souks are big enough to get lost in. Many have entire streets devoted to one particular craft or trade; brass, copper, leather, carpets, gold. Be curious, ask questions. Try haggling. Observe how many traders take credit cards and, if so, which ones are most favoured.

But even more than markets, people love to read of the food and wine of a country, of local dishes and specialities, from reindeer steaks to conch fritters, haggis to turtle pie. Novelists are particularly good at describing how food was served and the setting which accompanied a meal. In Ruth Prawer Jhabvala's *Heat and Dust*, set in India, 'Olivia's eyes lit up as she was led into the dining room and saw beneath the chandeliers the long, long table laid with a Sèvres dinner service, silver, crystal, flowers, candelabras, pomegranates, pineapples, and little bowls of crystallised fruits'.

Colette, the French novelist, was a reluctant traveller but fell in love with Morocco and, quite obviously, the food:

'Azul . . . placed before us pale girdle cakes soaked in sugared butter and sprinkled with almonds; pigeons bathed in succulent juice with green olives, chick-peas melting in flour, sweet onions; chickens buried under fresh beans with wrinkled skins and lemon, cooked and re-cooked and reduced to a savoury purée'.

Readers are also anxious to learn about the wines or beers of a country, and the local eating habits and customs. A good ethnic restaurant or one with famous (or infamous) associations which you have sampled personally and can recommend is also worth mentioning. Always try to find out where the locals eat rather than the tourists. Airline staff living and working abroad for a British company are invariably knowledgeable about characterful restaurants which no tourist could ever find without 'insider' knowledge. Getting staff to reveal them, however, especially if they suspect it may be for publication, is another matter.

Take part in local activities if you get the opportunity. Visit a funfair, for example, and watch how the locals enjoy themselves. How does it compare with funfairs at home? Do they sell hot-dogs and candy-floss or strange, unidentifiable items from their stands? Do people throw their discarded litter to the ground or carefully take it to a litter bin? Are the carousels decorated like ours? What is the music like – raucous Western pop or the equally raucous and monotonous wails of the East? Are they held in daylight or only in the evenings? At home, jumble sales, car boot sales and Granny's Attic Markets are equally entertaining and very good copy.

You may not want to spend vast sums on the theatre when the play is in a foreign language, but there are always exceptions. The Pyynikin open-air theatre in Tampere, Finland, where the backdrop stays put and the audience is revolved, offers a unique experience. Ballet, often held in a splendid opera house, can be enjoyed regardless of language. Circuses, too, do not require a knowledge of a foreign tongue and in a country such as Hungary, for instance, can be so very different from a circus at home as to be a totally new experience.

Audience reaction, too, can be worth writing about, as indeed can the way the audience behaves in the interval – is it subdued, does it form an orderly queue at the bar or indulge in a free-for-all? What is there to eat and drink? How are people dressed – are they shabby or old-fashioned, do they wear designer labels, silk and satin or crimplene and hand-knits? Hairstyles also offer a clue to the sophistication, or lack of it, of an audience, especially at an opera.

Cultivate first-hand experiences

Some cities such as Venice, Hamburg and Amsterdam lend themselves to waterborne sightseeing and excursions by motor boat and steamer, others to getting around by bike. Whether the local means of travel is camel, jeep or, in the case of a cliff-top monastery, by donkey, try to sample the thrills, the excitement and possibly even the terror at first-hand rather than through the reactions of a friend or colleague – the resultant copy will carry much more conviction.

Keep your readers in mind

A country's past, be it peaceful or tragic, eventful or uneventful, has helped to shape its present and will inevitably influence its future. Try to learn as much as you can about its history, particularly recent history, so that you can interpret it to your readers in the light of your present-day experiences.

But although you may personally be besotted with the history of a country or a city, remember that many of your readers will not care a fig for events which happened before they were born. They want to know what is happening today – what shows to see, the trendy places to eat, where to buy bargain china, designer clothes, souvenirs. Remember Carnaby Street? At one time it seemed that the entire world wanted to visit it and whether you were Italian, French, American or Japanese, you had only to return home with a Carnaby Street mug or wearing a Carnaby Street tee shirt to be accorded the kind of reverence shown to Muslims who have made the pilgrimage to Mecca.

Department stores provide good copy, but best of all are those shops that are still to be found in cities such as Lisbon and Budapest – shops with wooden floors, long mahogany counters, old-fashioned courtesy and those pneumatic cylinders for sending money off to the cashier high in her office at the back of the shop.

But it takes time to seek out the most characterful shops and time is always in short supply. Early closing (or a guide who gets uptight when you announce you'd rather see the local Harrods than visit an obscure museum) can conspire against you. It is better to plan a visit to a particular shop or shops from the very beginning, find out opening times, and be firm that this is one of your priorities than leave it to chance, hoping that you can squeeze it in between visiting the castle and the cathedral.

Don't despise a quick sortie round a lowly supermarket, either: readers enjoy comparing their local supermarkets with those in neighbouring towns, and are no less curious about how a supermarket in downtown Miami compares with their local Sainsbury's. At the very least, they give an insight into the standard of living in the neighbourhood. Confine your notes to a brief sentence or two, however, unless you have made some very remarkable or amusing discoveries among the shelves. Contrasts and comparisons are the red corpuscles of a travel article but are tiresome when too laboured or contrived.

Much as one would like to see inside the houses one passes, to see how they are furnished and how the owners live, in the normal course of events a stranger without contacts is unlikely to be invited into a home and share the life of the family for a few hours. It is, however, always worth while enquiring at the local tourist office if there are any home visit schemes in the area. The USA, Germany and Scandinavian countries are particularly good at operating such schemes, matching families with similar interests and jobs; the Japanese, too, have a 'Strangers into Friends' programme.

Animal interest

Animals invariably make good copy, domestic animals no less than the exotic creatures of the jungle. Mention dogs lolling around in the dust and scavenging in back-street dustbins and readers get the feel of a Mexican street scene; write of a uniformed chauffeur walking a poodle with a diamond-studded collar and readers recognise a not unfamiliar sight in Palm Beach.

Encounters with creepy-crawlies, however unpleasant, shouldn't be omitted from your copy either. Few places are perfect, and if a reader has a fear of spiders then obviously they would rather have advance warning. But things that creep, scud and scurry don't just occur in the jungles of this world. You are much more likely to be attacked by mosquitoes than by alligators in the Florida Everglades and I have encountered large land crabs scuttling around our hotel garden in Martinique. They – or their close relations – subsequently featured on the menu and, needless to say, in articles too.

A frog, for instance, played a leading – and witty – role in a *Daily Telegraph* article by Lucy Edward about a very grand Italian hotel:

> As the setting sun disappeared, the hotel frog started croaking. . . . The frog, which was typically, volubly Italian, was not to the manager's taste. After ten deafening minutes of amphibian love-songs echoing off polished marble, the diminutive culprit was discovered on a lily pad in the ornamental pond and gently returned to the wilds of the mountainside as we sat down to dinner. How glad I was that the Italians don't eat frogs' legs. It would have been like eating the band.

Be enterprising

Be enterprising; try to see those parts of a town or country which the tourist seldom sees. Package tourists to Cairo, for instance, see the celebrated sights such as the Pyramids and the Cairo Museum before being flown on to Luxor and Aswan. Few have time to visit the 'City of the Dead', the Eastern cemetery where an entire community lives in and amongst the tombs (some of which even sprout television aerials) and where the families of the deceased make regular visits for picnics.

Museums are of variable value to the travel writer and a matter of personal judgment. At best they can be a quick way of appreciating the history of an era or area, at worst they can be a waste of time. Many museums can be dazzling, their exhibits easily prompting half-a-dozen brilliant ideas (or so at least it appears at the time). Others can be tedious, badly presented, and lack labels explaining what the various items are, still less their provenance. As a quick rule of thumb, specialised museums, particularly museums devoted to cars and trains, usually arouse more reader interest than general museums.

Photographers frequently revisit a particular site or building at varying times of day to photograph it under different light conditions – the changing effects of light on a seascape or building can be quite stunning. One has only to remember the sunsets of Florida's Key West, or the Taj Mahal, incomparable by day but even more haunting by moonlight, to realise that what holds true for photographers can be useful advice for writers too.

Look up

Writers should also emulate artists and look upwards; the sky with scudding clouds or fat and fleecy cumulus is an important ingredient in country landscapes. In novels it helps establish atmosphere, something the tiro travel writer concentrating on country rambles often overlooks. In cities, it is easy to be so preoccupied taking notes that you forget to look up at the skyline, yet it can be every bit as busy and fascinating in its own way as events at street level. In a recent article on Madrid, for instance, E. S. Turner wrote: 'Mysteriously, the Arch of Independence has beckoning females, possibly winged, sitting as it were side-saddle along the parapet, with bare legs dangling; a welcome change from those rows of robed philosphers teetering precariously on the roofline.'

Local sayings are like salt and pepper

To be saleable, a travel article needs much more than facts, and travel writers are always on the alert for odd facts and legends which can spice up the current article or be noted for the future. My own notebook contains such disparate notes as:

Parma in Italy claims to have the world's most beautiful women.

'Haole', the Hawaiian word for foreigner, translates into 'someone who talks too much'.

The Turks have a proverb: 'God keep us from too little food and too much wine.'

In Florida, gumbo-limbo trees are called 'tourist trees' because of their peeling red skin.

Tuscany gets so many English visitors that it has been nicknamed 'Chiantishire'.

Assyrians call pearls 'fishes eyes'.

The Chinese call us 'big noses' and claim we smell of milk.

Diamonds are water-repellent.

If you are based in a city, try at least one day-trip out into the surrounding countryside (or the local beach if there is one) for a change of pace. Similarly if you are based in the country, devote a day to visiting the nearest town. Keep a note of how you travelled, how long it took you, how much it cost, details which have invariably evaporated from memory by the time you come to write the article.

You don't need to jet to faraway places

Not least of the attractions of writing about travel is that it can take you to strange and exotic places, lead you into rare experiences. It can also lead you into bus journeys across Australia of mind-dulling monotony, tedious train journeys through New Mexico, wasted hours waiting for the rain to go off, and listening to interminable speeches in a language you can't begin to comprehend. That side of travel writing, though, is rarely emphasised, even though the result may be an empty notebook. The illusion persists that travel writing is only for those who travel adventurously or to faraway places, for those who can offer travel experiences out of reach of the writer who never travels beyond the British Isles.

But the same principles apply whether you are writing about York or New York, Dunoon or Delhi. The British Isles encompass not only famous cities and towns and villages of enormous character but great tracts of unpopulated countryside; hundreds of islands waiting to be explored from the Shetlands to the Scilly Isles; gardens such as Inverewe and Sissinghurst famed for their interest; ancient and unusual parish churches; stately homes and even pubs which were standing long before our great great-grandparents were born. There's no need to concentrate on the old and picturesque of course. How many people have experienced shark-fishing from Looe or are even aware that it's the shark-fishing capital of Britain? How many people know the Japanese are very keen on Beatrix Potter, that people visit Bradford especially to go on one of their curry tours or that there's an annual two-day Garlic Festival at Newport on the Isle of Wight complete with Garlic Queen and Vampire King? How many people know that Leicester has the highest concentration of Asian residents in Europe, the largest sari shop outside India and a Gujarati community where reputedly more gold is sold across the counter than anywhere in Europe? A good and perceptive travel writer can make readers just as keen and curious to visit his own particular corner of Britain as they are to visit, say, Bali or Bangkok.

If you doubt this, turn to novelists like Thomas Hardy or Laurie Lee's autobiography *Cider With Rosie*, full of evocative word pictures of the Cotswold countryside:

The whirr of the mower met us across the stubble, rabbits jumped like firecrackers about the fields, and the hay smelt crisp and sweet.

White roads, rutted by hooves and cartwheels, innocent of oil and petrol.

Mushrooms . . . buttoning the shaggy grass, found in the mists of September mornings with the wet threads of spiders on them.

and of a visit to the seaside:

Rousing smells of an invisible ocean astonished our land-locked nostrils; salt, and wet weeds, and fishy oozes; a sharp difference in every breath.

Is homework really necessary?

Many travel writers read as much about a destination before they leave home as they possibly can. Others prefer to arrive in a new country without any of the preconceptions which inevitably form through reading other people's impressions. It is often difficult to better a description of a place once a famous writer has already encapsulated it in a single phrase, easier to come up with something original if you haven't read previous descriptions. Having once heard Finland described as 'the land of liquid lace', for instance, I find myself helpless to improve on this felicitous phrase which seems to have permanently impressed itself on my mind. And John Betjeman's summation of Sydney Opera House as 'a rugby scrum of nuns' gets between the traveller and his notebook every time. Nevertheless, I belong to the read-all-you-can-before-you-go school of thought, and I particularly read guide books. It's frustrating to get back from a trip and discover that, if only you'd done your homework beforehand, you were close enough to a garden of exceptional beauty to visit it by local bus, and maddening to arrive at the art gallery you had planned to see the next time you were in Paris or Florence, only to find it shut.

Tackling the creative part

But it is when you get back from your travels, notebooks spilling over with colourful details, and maps, postcards and books to hand, that the first problems appear. You have so much disparate material that you don't know where to start. The place just hides there, waiting – 'defying you to reduce its multiformity to a few paragraphs' as the novelist Paddy Kitchen neatly observed.

The hardest part of writing a travel article is often the opening paragraph. There's the dramatic approach: 'It was the kind of storm in which sea captains lash themselves to the wheel'; 'My arrival in Anchorage was preceded by a volcanic eruption and a murder'; or an opening which captures the tone and sets the pace for the rest of the article:

> 'There was a gust of laughter from the back of our 'plane. "I guess they must be Southerners," explained my neighbour from New Orleans. "We're a much more relaxed people here".'

Sometimes the entire spirit of the place can be encapsulated in the first paragraph of an article, as exemplified in a travel piece in the *Daily Telegraph* by David Twiston Davies to celebrate Dublin's 1000th birthday:

> The trick on arriving in Ireland is to adjust your mind, not your watch. For while in London each minute is to be snatched, crammed and husbanded, in Dublin 60 seconds represent a strangely elastic period which should be enjoyed, savoured and, if somehow lost, tacked on to the end of all those other essential matters begging your attention.

The commonest fault when first writing travel articles is the school essay syndrome – 'we went to the beach in the morning and then we had lunch in a beach cabin and then went to the shops in the afternoon'. The result is pure tedium for the reader. Don't expect or even try to use all the material which you have collected – having too much rather than too little enables you to be selective rather than having to resort to padding.

Whatever your subject matter, try to inject a bit of humour into it, like the chap who was faced with sampling kangaroo meat in a London restaurant and reflected that, after all, to Australians, kangaroos were nothing but 'sheep which hop'. Or like the writer who was driving through Morocco and wanted to stop at an oasis: 'I paid a small boy to watch the car (the Moroccan equivalent of feeding a parking meter)'.

Whether to write in the first or third person depends very much on your market. While the third person is generally more acceptable, the first person is often more effective for recounting trekking, horse-riding, sailing and other action holidays, as the opening paragraph of Peter Chambers' article *Motley Crewing* illustrates: 'The boom-boom started at 2 a.m. and it sounded like bombardment. I woke up, wondering where I was, cracked my head against the deckhead, and remembered – on a small boat.'

Having started this chapter with advice on being creative, it is perhaps best to end on a note of caution. Over-creativity may lead you into 'improving' your copy by exaggerating or even making something up. Resist the temptation. You are writing about a country, a destination as you observe it at a particular time in its history, and owe it to your readers to tell it as it is; if you feel you must gloss it up or romanticise it, fine, but turn it into fiction set against the background of that particular country and don't pass it off as a travel article.

Be sure that the trips and excursions you write about will still be in existence by the time they get into print, and that the reader can duplicate the experiences you write about. Check, for instance, that the trip by camel up to the volcano in Lanzarote is not being discontinued and replaced by a bus next month.

Don't carry your prejudices, hang-ups or preconceptions with you, be they social or political. And never be so insensitive as to write as if you were superior to the people you travel amongst.

Travel writers also owe it to their readers to get the facts right. This aim is not as obvious or achievable as it may seem, thanks to guides, guide books and reference books seldom being in agreement. Conflicting information may come from many sources and checking facts involves hours of research, so with a deadline coming up fast there is always the temptation to take a chance. Inevitably there will be someone out there who will write to you (or worse, your editor), ready to niggle, complain or crow that you misspelt Uffizi or were a mile short when you quoted the length of the White Nile.

If you are doubtful about the spelling of local names, whether to use Tokyo or Tokio, Teheran or, as it is always spelt in Iran, Tehran, it matters less which one you choose than that you are consistent all through the article or book. One advantage of working on a word processor is its 'search and find' facility which can ensure consistency even when, half way through a book, you discover you have used Tehran in one paragraph and Teheran in the next.

But although you will undoubtedly take the craftsmanship of travel writing seriously, don't make such heavy weather of the techniques that you lose the kind of spontaneity and humour which the late Gerald Durrell's reaction to a stranger illustrates so delightfully: 'A polite young man approached us wearing a smart grey uniform and on his head what appeared to be a large Persian cat lying somnolent and supine. This, on closer inspection, turned out to be his elegant fur hat.' (*Durrell in Russia*)

6
Writing Travel Articles

A travel writer is almost invariably a person who works for a newspaper or magazine either as one of their staff, usually as a travel editor or travel correspondent, or a freelance working for as many publications as possible without being under contract to any particular one.

Unless you are already a journalist and are suddenly catapulted into the heady position of travel editor, you will almost certainly be starting out by submitting travel articles to newspapers and magazines 'on spec'. If you are successful, and have a sufficient number of travel articles published, then you too can lay claim to being a freelance travel writer.

There is a pecking order in staff positions, with travel editors at the top – a powerful position in that they can commission articles and have the cream of all the invitations which come in. Many publications have travel correspondents rather than travel editors. A correspondent usually works on a retainer basis and contributes all the travel articles personally. While travel editors frequently commission most of the material they use, travel correspondents seldom have a budget which allows them to commission articles as an alternative to writing them themselves.

Both travel editors and travel correspondents are invariably overwhelmed with invitations from airlines, overseas governments, tourist bodies, hotels, tour operators and public relations companies to visit their part of the world, to stay at their hotel, travel by their airline, stay in their camping site. Inevitably it isn't possible to accept all the invitations which come along and travel editors are in the happy position of being able to arrange their own visits to an area they want to write about and charge expenses to their newspaper or publication. Freelancers, on the other hand, frequently find they have to write several articles on the one travel destination to make it worth their while accepting the trip in the first place. Marketing your articles to an editor can take as much time and skill as writing them in the first place.

Travel editors always have to balance out the types of holiday included in their pages to suit their readership. On the whole they are very even-handed about it, although if the travel editor is particularly keen on outdoor activities who can blame him (or her) for giving riding, sailing and walking more column space than, say, beach holidays, or the travel editor whose weakness is for skiing giving more prominence to skiing resorts than winter sun spots? Astute freelancers who study the papers' travel columns every week will soon detect any bias towards a particular type of holiday, and exploit it if they can.

On most nationals the travel editors simply can't accept all the invitations which come their way so the invitations are farmed out, often to other members of the staff, and usually – but not inevitably – to match their interests.

Some magazines are less scrupulous about this and will post less important invitations on the office notice board so that anyone on the staff, even the editorial secretaries, can be representing the publication. If the resultant article is particularly good, this is fine; a new talent has been discovered. If it is bad it never gets beyond the wastepaper basket, which is sad, both for the person or group issuing the invitation and freelancers, who could have made good use of such an invitation if only they had received it first.

Writing as a freelance

Until they get established, freelancers have to make their own opportunities. Once your name appears regularly it is entirely possible that you will start receiving invitations in your own right. This solves the problem of what to write about but not the problem of where to send an article. If you have been invited on a press trip you will almost inevitably find yourself in the company – and in competition with – half-a-dozen others all writing for the same market.

If you are specialising in a particular market, try to get your name on as many of the public relations companies' press lists as possible. Although much of the resultant press bumph is destined for the nation's wastepaper baskets, it is frequently useful as a source of ideas, building up background files, and the occasional invitation.

Interpreting the readership

Studying potential markets is as essential as keeping up your ideas file. If you are a regular reader of the *Daily Telegraph*, for instance, you will have a very good idea not only of the style but of the contents of the travel articles. Being a regular reader, you can safely assume that other readers are roughly in the same financial bracket, have a similar educational background and that the travel editor would be receptive to a little history, details about the country's food and wine and references to exciting exhibits in local museums in any articles you considered submitting.

Could you be so confident, though, about the travel pages of tabloids such as the *Sun* or the *Daily Mirror*, however, if you weren't a regular reader? Although it is very likely that the educational background of their readers is not in the same class as the quality papers, it isn't always safe to assume that their financial status can't match that of the more upmarket papers. Readers of these particular tabloids often have a much higher disposable income than readers of *The Times*, for instance. Since their money isn't tied up in heavy mortgages and school fees, they have more money to spend on holidays, fewer inhibitions about spending it, and are as likely to contemplate a holiday in Barbados or Thailand, the Seychelles or Mauritius as any *Times* reader.

You may, however, find it more difficult to emulate the style of the tabloids than the *Telegraph, Times, Guardian* or *Independent*. Short sentences, each sentence a separate paragraph, sound remarkably easy to write until you try to condense your impressions of a city into 200 words, or a weekend in the West Country into 150.

The age of a newspaper's readership is of considerable importance to its publishers, for this is a powerful tool in influencing potential advertisers. While the readers of the *Daily Telegraph*, for instance, may predominantly appear to be middle-aged, remember that the publishers are trying – and succeeding – in attracting a younger readership. This is reflected in their editorial pages, and in the travel pages no less than in other columns. *The Times*, too, has made great efforts to attract younger readers, and is less solemn than it used to be. Keep this in mind when writing your article, and if you are well above the age of the readership, don't give it away consciously or unconsciously by using phrases like 'In my day . . .' or by making value judgments about how shocked you were to find the beach was full of topless females.

In the magazine world, age is even more important, with the style and contents closely targetted to the interests – and income – of men and women in quite narrow age groups. Many of the newer magazines for women which are now proliferating on the bookstands are aimed at younger women – many of the magazines, in fact, set out to appeal specifically to the 18–24 age group, so it is of little use submitting an article heavy with comments on museums and architecture when the readers are primarily inter-ested in beaches, discos, bright lights and where to meet the opposite sex.

The solution is to find the newspapers and magazines whose style you are comfortable with and whose travel pages reflect your own interests and priorities, and which are authoritative enough to influence your personal choice of destination – the type of travel articles which make you say 'I'd like to go there', 'I'd like to do that'.

Beware of travel articles which appear to be written to a formula, and extol the virtues of whatever place they are visiting this week in precisely the same terms as last week's article, regardless of the fact that they are describing places as far apart as Majorca and Thailand. Be very wary, too, of publications where the travel articles are high on hype and invariably overwritten. Rather like the theatre critics whose rave reviews are splashed over the bill-boards, it is hard for the normal reader to suspend credulity to such an extent that he believes everything was quite so brilliant/wonderful/perfect and paradisaical.

Submitting travel articles

Having done your market research, you may have found at least three possible markets for the article you have in mind. Do you write it first and send it in with the photographs, do you send the editor a query letter, or should you phone up the editor direct, tell him you are off to Australia, staying on the Great Barrier Reef, and would he be interested in an article?

Since editors are invariably over the top of their heads with work, I would only telephone if I knew him/her well, and knew that it was the kind of material that interested them. It is not unheard of for six travel writers all suggesting an article on Hong Kong to ring up on the same day, particularly if there is a press trip in the offing and each of them has received an invitation in the morning's post. The race often goes to the one who is fastest to the phone. But a travel editor will never assign an article to an unknown writer who rings up to say, 'I've been invited to Australia, is there anything I can do for you there?' And as travel editors spend a considerable time out of the country rather than sitting at a desk you may not be able to get an instant decision, even if you are on first name terms with them.

Unless they know you well, most editors will not give you a definite commission, but will say that they are interested in seeing the finished article. They may possibly give you the optimum length, which is of great assistance.

If you are totally unknown, sending in the finished article is definitely your best route into print. Seldom does a trip turn out entirely as planned and the material you gather may be too thin to sustain a long article. The emphasis may change when you have to go a different route, and you may make on-the-spot discoveries that you never knew existed. If you have been commissioned to write an article, you have more or less to stick to the itinerary you originally outlined. If you are sending it in on spec then you have the freedom to change your mind about its structure and content half-a-dozen times before you post it.

Query letters

Alternatively you can write a query letter first – basically a letter of enquiry giving the salient points about the destination you are about to visit or have just visited, and asking if the editor would be interested. If the editor doesn't know you, include a few lines on your writing credentials, provided, that is, that they are germane to the article. It is surprising how many people think it necessary to include totally superfluous details, such as their marital status (or history).

Don't write things like 'I am only a housewife but you may be interested in the once-in-a-lifetime trip I took to America last month'. Be positive; why was your trip there different from anyone else's trip to the States? It may have been a once-in-a-lifetime trip for you, but many travel writers spend large chunks of their year there and know some states much better than they do London. Your job is to convince the editor that yours is a special story because you visited the National Peanut Festival at Dothan, Alabama, for instance, or travelled all the way from New Orleans to Los Angeles on the top deck of a double decker train. You must have an angle, and the better the angle, the better your chance of interesting an editor. Never begin your query letter with 'I've never read your magazine but I thought you might be interested in . . .' You should be thoroughly familiar with the type of material regularly published there, and be able to suggest a subject which hasn't already been covered in the issues you have studied.

Have definite ideas to put in your letter: don't expect the editor to give you an assignment just because you are going to Mexico – only Lord Snowdon or someone of equal prominence could get off with that. If, however, you say you are going to Acapulco to do a story on 'High divers and low flyers' – i.e. the tourists who go parasailing and the locals who make those spectacular dives from the cliffs into a little square of sea – that is a different matter. You have to write such a good query letter that the editor wonders how he ever got along without an article on this very subject. It is up to you to say what you can do for the publication, not the editor's place to ask.

The purpose of a query letter is to establish that there isn't an article on the same subject already in stock or commissioned. Once the editor has agreed an interest – and given you a deadline if possible – then he will not accept one on this topic even if it arrives on the following day from an unexpected source. You have won yourself some breathing space. All you have to do now is make sure you write and send in the article as quickly as possible. If you don't, you will be discredited as a professional travel writer.

It can take several hours to plan a query letter and it may take several hours or even days of research to get the relevant information you need before you can compile your letter. Even so, confine it to two or three paragraphs – never put so much into it that it runs over to a second page. Finish with a few of your credentials for writing the article. Do not send cuttings at this stage – if the editor is interested in your suggestion he may ask to see examples of your published work. If you haven't any published work to show, don't query – send in the completed manuscript.

Although travel editors on the nationals get dozens of travel ideas and suggestions every week, less widely known magazines and publications aren't so fortunate, particularly controlled circulation magazines where a professional readership is interested in the travel page as consumers rather than contributors. Here a query letter may be more effective if it contains multiple suggestions rather than just a single idea for a destination piece.

It is, of course, difficult to do this unless one has travelled sufficiently widely to be able to suggest half-a-dozen different destinations, all with varying angles. Some freelance travel writers undoubtedly travel so much that they are able to send out a list of a dozen or more suggestions every few months – all freshly experienced material, too.

Amongst so many ideas, there is almost bound to be at least one which hasn't been covered before and which sparks off sufficient interest in the editor's mind to prompt a go-ahead. Like Premium Bonds, where the holders are said to stand a greater chance of winning the more bonds they hold, I believe that the more ideas you have to offer, the better your chances of having one accepted.

But keep the suggestions short – two or three lines at the most in a query letter containing multiple ideas. You can devote more space – a short paragraph perhaps – if you are querying a single idea for a travel piece, but make sure you keep the total letter well within one page – brevity will get you much further than length at this stage.

Keeping up with travel trends

From the point of view of marketing your articles, it is always a good idea to keep up with trends, remembering that as a travel writer you may even be influencing them. No less than hemlines, destinations go in and out of fashion. Turkey, Greece, Vietnam, have all in their turn been flavour of the month, but next year ... who knows?

Depending once again on your market, keep your eye on the top ten popularity lists published by the tour operators as an indication of where people are going for their holidays abroad. Kuoni publish one on long-haul destinations, and tour operators such as Travelscene a European city one, with Paris invariably heading the list. Again, the conference market has quite a different set of preferred destinations, and participants tend to vote on an international basis rather than a purely local one. The criteria are different too, and tend to be based on the facilities available for hosting large conferences rather than sandy-versus-stony beaches, the number of hours of sunshine and the other preoccupations of someone who is there purely for recreation.

At home, the respective tourist offices for England, Scotland and Wales will give you the top ten most popular places in their countries, even the top ten most popular tourist attractions and stately homes. There is enormous rivalry among the owners of stately homes to get into the top ten, regarding this as a reflection of their marketing skills.

But it isn't just destinations and countries which go in and out of fashion. Even different types of scenery have their day. It is difficult to realise nowadays, for instance, that at one time travellers avoided the French Riviera, and preferred the scenery of the Mount Cenis pass. But even when the Riviera started to become fashionable in the 19th century it failed to enrapture Swinburne who managed to sound singularly disenchanted about it:

> A calcined, scalped ... leprous, blotched, mangy, grimy, parboiled country WITHOUT trees, water, grass, fields – WITH blank, beastly senseless olive and orange trees ... it is infinitely like hell on earth

and one looks for tails among the people. And such females with hunched bodies and crooked necks carrying tons on their heads and looking like Death taken seasick.

Mark Twain, in spite of putting the Mississippi on the literary map, must have undone a lot of his good work – at least as far as tourism was concerned – by remarking that the famous iron railings of the Old French Quarter of New Orleans had little 'architectural value except in cemeteries'. And Charles Lamb complained that 'We have been dull at Worthing one summer, duller at Brighton another, dullest at Eastbourne a third, and are now doing penance at Hastings!' Were he alive today, I doubt if Charles Lamb would have much future as a travel writer.

Scotland, at one time so vastly inaccessible except by sea, suddenly came into fashion at the end of the Napoleonic wars, helped not only by the growth of the railways and the novels of Sir Walter Scott but by Queen Victoria, whose interest in Balmoral could well be said to have put Royal Deeside on the tourist map.

Nowadays it tends to be film and TV programmes which put places on the map, thus providing a useful angle for alert travel writers. Suffolk, Amersham, Yorkshire and Oxford have all benefitted from pilgrimages made by tourists as a result of seeing a particular film or TV series. Coach tours in particular are very quick to exploit this market.

At any given time politics, an outbreak of the plaque, cholera or typhoid or terrorist activities may mean your article is put on a back burner. There are times when you just have to be philosophical. Don't pester the editor when the crisis is over to know how soon it will be used. It may have passed its sell-by date by then. A gentle reminder, however, after a discreet interval, may help to ensure that your article will live to appear another day.

Get your timing right

Most of the quality nationals now publish a separate weekend section on Saturdays devoted to things like leisure pursuits, travel, personal finance and criticism, which helps to guarantee a minimum number of travel articles throughout the year. In the past travel articles tended to appear on a seasonal basis, were very thin on the ground in the summer months and filled page after page in January.

There is still a 'season' for travel articles but it has grown considerably from the days when pages fat with enticing features on the pleasures and excitements of foreign parts started appearing immediately after Christmas and lasted until the end of January. Now the season starts earlier and lasts longer, with heavy advertising – and therefore an increased number of editorial pages – from November until the spring of the following year, reaching its peak in January.

January is also the month when a considerable number of travel supplements appear, and images of sunny climates, blonde beaches and waving palm trees are at their most potent. It is also the time when ski buffs are highly susceptible to reading about new ski resorts and terrain.

The proliferating number of colour magazines which accompany the Sunday papers – from *You* to *The Sunday Times Magazine* – also devote themselves to travel as soon as Christmas is over. They cover travel not as a regular feature – in fact it may only be tackled intermittently or once or twice a year at the most – but when they do cover it, they do it with enthusiasm, often devoting the entire contents of the magazine to it.

Each of the colour magazines has a separate staff from the accompanying newspapers, which means a different travel editor will be commissioning the travel articles. It also means a greater number of opportunities for different styles and approaches to travel. The fact that last year the travel articles were all written by well-known television personalities or that all the articles centred on fashionable beach resorts doesn't mean that the same formula will be used this year, and shouldn't deter you from approaching the magazines with your own ideas if you feel they represent the ideal market for the articles you have in mind.

Articles should be submitted at sensible times. Put yourself in the position of the travel editor: would you want to see an article on autumn breaks appearing in your January post-bag with a covering note asking for a quick decision? Dafter things have happened. It will get the quickest decision possible, i.e. be sent back immediately without even being read.

Since the travel pages of the nationals often work months ahead and magazines six to eight weeks ahead of publication, allow at least another month on top of this for your work to be considered. Submit seasonal articles about three months ahead (four for Christmas travel features), but not too far ahead.

Nowadays many editors concentrate on themes, with every travel article in a particular issue devoted to different facets of that theme, whether it is cycling tours, farm holidays, cruising, skiing or revolves round one particular country such as India or Australia. This approach is frequently dictated by the newspaper's advertising department, which likes to know the contents of future issues well in advance, the better to sell advertising space.

In many ways this editorial policy affords the freelance contributor a better chance of getting an article accepted. The one you have submitted – say an unusual angle on Belgium – may not have been strong enough to stand by itself but fits in as snugly as a jigsaw piece in a theme issue.

From time to time, some national newspapers publicise forthcoming themes but this is very haphazard and you may have to search in advertising spaces to find these elusive details. The snag with themes is that by the time they are publicised it may well be too late to submit for that year. If you read on August 1st that the August 8th issue will be devoted to France then it is certainly much too late to send in your article on 'Barging through Burgundy'. On the other hand, if you notice that the October 8th issue will be on a waterborne theme, then it is worth sending your article in on spec. A deluge of advertisers attracted by the theme may well make extra editorial pages feasible at the last minute and gain your article a welcome acceptance.

Because of the heavy number of travel pages carried in the winter months, the autumn is a particularly hectic period for travel writers, who are kept busy supplying the demand for articles required by newspapers by November 1st.

Winter is the time when readers are most looking forward to summer and are particularly receptive to the destinations they read about in newspapers and magazines. There is also the forthcoming Christmas season to cater for – should readers celebrate Christmas abroad and, if so, where? A traditional Christmas here at home in a country inn is appealing, but round-up articles giving the ambience of half-a-dozen country inns throughout the country, their log fires and seasonal food, diversions like Christmas carols in the church next door and the local Boxing Day hunt, need to be written the previous summer. I have been invited to Christmas parties publicising these seasonal activities as early as July 6th.

The three types of travel article

Most types of travel articles fall into three main patterns, and the 'round-up' is one of the easiest to write. Once you have up-to-date material in front of you, this type of article almost writes itself, for it is more a matter of selection and variety than a test of literary skill. Spring and autumn breaks particularly lend themselves to this treatment but it can also be a useful way of presenting an article on where half-a-dozen celebrities like to spend their Christmas holidays, for example, or where they spent their honeymoon, even their favourite bars throughout the world, and why.

The most usual type of travel article is the straightforward 'This is the destination, this is what it looks like, this is what it feels like', and it is the pattern favoured by most newspapers and magazines.

The third type, first person anecdotal stories, are less easy to place since they come perilously close to sounding like an ego trip if you aren't careful. Magazines which use them, such as *High Life*, tend to commission them from people like Terry Wogan, Michael Parkinson and Gloria Hunniford rather than unknown freelancers.

Find an intriguing title

A good title gets your article off to a favourable reception as far as the editor is concerned, even if a sub-editor comes along and alters it before publication. Sub-editors on newspapers are notorious for altering copy, even putting in clichés where there were none before, and leaving out what you personally regarded as a particularly vital sentence. Titles may be shortened or expanded at the last moment because of the overall layout of the entire page, but at least you are over the first hurdle – getting your work accepted in the first place.

An apt title frequently suggests itself from the body of the copy – a phrase which seems to sum up the entire article may jump out at you without any mental exertion on your part such as 'Look before you Book' for an article on travel videos. Punning titles like 'Round the Isles in Eighty Bays', a story about island-hopping in Greece, are much favoured by the *Guardian* and certain glossies, and their popularity has now spread to many of the heavies, whose recent titles have included 'Going for the Maine Attractions', 'The Qualities of Mersey', 'Wizard Oz' and 'Let Yourself Goa'. Most people resort to alliterative titles like Happy Hamburg, Thrilling Thailand and Bewitching Bali when desperate. I know that it can easily absorb an entire day, off and on, trying out alternative titles in your head, but better that than sending out your precious manuscript with a banal title.

Writing down all the possible title combinations you can think of, switching them round, trying them back to front and upside down if necessary often helps to arrive at an intriguing solution. A touch of lateral thinking does wonders in initiating both titles and subjects to write about.

Taking the title of a well-known book, film or play and altering it slightly to suit your article is another obvious solution, which has the merit of endowing your article with an instantly recognisable reference – a title like 'Treasure Islands', for instance. The snag here is that you can't keep on using the same title over and over again in a lifetime devoted to writing about islands, and have to come up with something new on every occasion.

How to judge the fee

If your main concern is to write for money (some publications pay so little that their fee wouldn't even cover the cost of mailing postcards home to friends let alone relatives), then your market research will have to be very concentrated. Even if you would be so elated to see your name over a travel article in *The Times* that you would gladly allow them to publish it for nothing, it is only being professional to expect something for your work.

The Times gives you prestige and pays well; as a general rule, the higher the circulation of a publication the higher the fee you receive, which is why the *Sun*, the *News of the World* and the *Daily Mirror* also pay well. Although you probably have a rough idea already of the circulation figures of the nationals – whether they are above the million mark or below it – you can confirm these by consulting a copy of *Benn's Media*, which should be in the reference section of your local library. This gives the circulation figures of every newspaper, provincial as well as national, in the country, as well as magazines. Their payment cheques, however, can't just be judged on circulation figures alone – often the more prestigious the magazine the lower the fees are. If you do succeed in getting a travel article in *Vogue* or *Harper's*, however, great is the kudos even if the cheque is smaller than you might expect from *The Times*, *The Sunday Times* or the *Sun*.

Payment for an article is generally expressed in terms of so many pounds per 1000 words and £100–150 per 1000 words is the general average for many magazines, while newspapers such as the *Daily Telegraph* and *The Sunday Times* pay two or three times as much, and certain publications given away free in London pay – very reluctantly – at the rate of only £30 per 1000.

Lucky is the contributor who is paid on acceptance – i.e. within a few weeks of an editor signifying his/her willingness to publish the article you have recently submitted. Most payments are made 'on publication' – a euphemism for 'six weeks following publication' in some cases. Nor should you imagine that because your article has been accepted it will be in print the following day, week, or even year, so don't start celebrating the moment you hear the good news.

Since most newspapers appear on a daily basis, the public thinks that they are made up the night before. This is largely the result of seeing too many old Hollywood films – the green eyeshade syndrome, the hold-the-front-page urgency of the newspaper world. Apart from the news and the welcome appearance of last-minute advertisements, other pages such as travel and non-topical features are often stockpiled for months and even years. An article that has been commissioned in January one year from a regular contributor who is off to ski in Aspen, Colorado, may well be held over for publication until January of the following year.

Magazines are often worse, and publish travel articles they have been holding on to for a year or more without first asking the writer to check that the basic facts haven't gone out of date in the interval. If payment for an article is on publication, then inflation will inevitably have nibbled some of the value of your cheque away by the time you receive it.

If, on the other hand, the publication has changed hands or folded altogether, you may never receive payment at all. If the publishers are reputable they should – ideally – pay you the full fee for the article they commissioned, or, at the very least, what is known as a 'kill' fee. This is approximately half the fee you would have received had the article been published, and as you are free to submit the article to another publication you may do rather better from it than you originally intended.

Commissioning letters

When a new magazine, particularly one which isn't well-known or established, gives you a go-ahead on a suggestion you have sent in, it is always advisable to ask for a commissioning letter. This will confirm that you have been asked to write, say, a 1500 word article on Andalucia by 20th August for a fee of £200. The length of the article is important, as is the copy date and the fee. If the magazine subsequently folds without your article being published then at least you have written proof of a commission. It isn't as comforting as a cheque, but a well-known publishing house might just buy the title of the one which has folded, and honour its debts to contributors.

Many of the nationals pay exceedingly well for photographs, especially if a photograph has been reproduced over several columns. Payment depends on size and the number of photographs used. On the other hand, many provincial papers accept the photograph as part of the article and don't pay anything, so it is advisable to check first with the publication to find out what their policy is.

Even this doesn't avoid the maddening situation where you have gone to the trouble and expense of sending out your own photographs only to find that free handout photographs have been used to save the publication money.

There was a time when certain magazines and newspapers were closed shops and articles would only be accepted when the contributor was a member of the NUJ. These days have gone and the present climate positively encourages freelance contributors who have something worthwhile to write about. Aim high, however, and don't be afraid to submit an article on your travel experiences to *The Times*, the *Guardian*, the *Daily Telegraph* or *The Sunday Times*, for instance, if your article is aimed at this market. The travel editor will judge your article on its qualities, regardless of whether he or she has ever met you, heard of you or knows of you. The opportunities are undoubtedly there. All you have to do is go for them.

7
Writing Travel Books

As I remarked in the chapter 'Motives', there has seldom been such an appetite for travel as there is today, nor, since the golden years of travel writing from the pens of Freya Stark and Peter Fleming, has there been such an appetite for reading about other people's travels.

Whether travel writing is in or out of fashion, of course, matters little to true travellers, who would pen their experiences in a strange country regardless of whether or not anyone would read them. Quite often, what is ultimately published as a travel book starts out as notes on a journey confided to a diary.

Write with style

The quality of a writer's style is important in writing a successful travel book. As Evelyn Waugh, reviewing Peter Fleming's *News from Tartary*, acknowledged, 'The very stuff of travel is not the dramatic incidents but rather the day to day routine ... the delays and uncertainties, the minor vexations – whole drab uneventful patches of sheer hard work and discontent. The way to make such experience fascinating for the reader is through sheer style.'

Norman Douglas thought that, 'The reader of a good travel book is entitled not only to an exterior voyage, to descriptions of scenery and so forth, but to an interior, a sentimental or temperamental voyage which takes place side by side with the outer one'. This was written before the days of television. The much acclaimed contemporary travel writer, Colin Thubron reckons that the travel book should be extinct by now, killed off by television:

> But of course precisely the opposite has happened. . . . The interaction between the author and his landscape explains, I believe, why parallel television ventures have failed to supersede the travel book. Not only is a film crew incapable of capturing those chance moments of intimacy so vital to the traveller, but the camera lens merely renders back to the viewer the world as he would see it himself if he were

standing in the camera's place. In a book, exactly the opposite happens. The reader, crucially, is seeing through the eyes of another – with his sensibility, his fears, his preferences.

There is a feeling that those who write autobiographical travel books are the élite of the travel writing world, and it is certainly true that while few people remember the name of the person who wrote the guide book that they found so invaluable in Turkey or in Russia, most people immediately recognise the names of Jan Morris, Bruce Chatwin, Colin Thubron, Jonathan Raban and Eric Newby as those of travel writers.

The rewards of writing a narrative travel book are not financial. Indeed, unless your name becomes a household one, the financial rewards are so low they probably wouldn't begin to cover Alan Whicker's credit card bills. What a book may lose in the financial stakes, however, is made up in terms of prestige, for a travel book tells a wide audience what *you* have done and seen. Other people come back from a fortnight in Tunisia and tell all their friends, colleagues, relatives and fellow commuters on the 8.05 a.m. of their experiences; a travel book writer comes back from six months in Cambodia, China or South America and shares his experience with an audience of several thousand, even more if his book should be chosen as 'A Book at Bedtime' for Radio 4.

There will always be armchair travellers, however much super-sonic aircraft shorten the journey to faraway places and however much exotic islands are packaged to make them more accessible, more hygienic, and cheaper to visit. Many travellers are armchair ones partly because they don't want their illusions destroyed; each of us needs a personal ShangriLa to retreat to. Even a country's warts can be happily accommodated in an illusion. Visiting it can spoil the dream for ever. Many myths have evolved from the pens of travellers and been perpetuated by later travellers and travel writers. Few people ever tell you how insignificant Cairo's Giza pyramids are, for instance, or Rio's Sugar Loaf Mountain, so stunning in photographs but much less impressive in reality.

And, let's face it, many people are content to be armchair travellers because they haven't the courage or the stamina to be a traveller of the adventurous type they admire, nor do they have the time or money.

For the most part, the autobiographical travel book is either the result of living in a foreign country for a long number of years, such as Arthur Grimble's account of living in the Pacific, *A Pattern of Islands*, or an account of a journey through strange (in the sense of entirely new to you) and preferably exotic lands and the chance encounters and experiences with people en route.

Time and inclination

But books of this type need time; time to take the journey in the first place, time to write about it. And money. A private income is useful, savings you can draw on while writing the book almost mandatory. Even in the poorer parts of the world, even in those places where barter takes the place of money, even among the most primitive tribes, you need money for food, for transport, even for clothing.

Some expenses continue while you are away, and you are not likely to be earning much for the time you are travelling unless you have been fortunate enough to land a commission to make a television documentary about the places you pass through, or writing about your trip is a spin-off from your main interest (like the Durrells in Russia). But breaks like this are unlikely to come the way of an unknown, unproven travel book writer.

On the plus side, setting out on your travels with the intention of writing a book about your experiences gives you the satisfaction of being a free spirit, going where you please, seeing the things which please you and not your readers, travelling how you will and without a timetable – unless, of course, you have signed a contract and have promised to write a book by a certain date, which is unlikely to happen first time out. Writing a travel book is almost the only type of travel writing where you don't have the pressures of thinking of your readers the whole time, and of what *they* want to know rather than what *you* want to find out.

You will need money, of course, but, apart from the highly industrialised countries, not nearly as much as you would living and working in Britain. Time is a difficult commodity to find but some people nowadays are able to take a three month sabbatical break from work; young people have time to fit in a trip overseas before going to college or university and, once there, have many opportunities for joining a university expedition or cheap travel to other countries. Patrick Leigh Fermor was only 18 when he made the journey from Holland to Constantinople that was to result in his famous book, *A Time of Gifts*. Even redundancy, traumatic as it is at the time, can provide you with the opportunity of a lump sum of money and a breathing space for achieving your childhood ambition – a trip up the Amazon, perhaps, a visit to Lhasa or the former headhunters of Toba.

Although it is pointless to set out on an ambitious project like crossing the Sahara or South America or exploring the course of the Nile and then run out of time or money when you are only halfway through, you can tailor your journey to the time you have available. True, Patrick Leigh Fermor took 1½ years on his journey to Constantinople but, on the other hand, Geoffrey Moorhouse's journey from Karachi to the North West Frontier of Pakistan took only three months and resulted in the book *To The Frontier*.

There are no set rules about this form of travel writing, which is why it is so appealing. You can travel how you will: Eric Newby travelled on foot, Gavin Young by boat, Colin Thubron by car, Dervla Murphy by bicycle, Geoffrey Moorhouse by camel and Robert Louis Stevenson, as we all know, travelled with a donkey.

Many people have moved from certain careers in the commercial or professional world into the uncertainty of travel writing. Eric Newby, one of Britain's best-known travel writers, worked as a buyer for a chain of dress shops before he took his famous *Short Walk in the Hindu Kush*.

The late Bruce Chatwin worked for Sotheby's for eight years, authenticating paintings. 'In the end I felt I might just as well be working for a rather superior funeral parlour. One's whole life seemed to be spent valuing for probate in the apartment of somebody recently dead ... I began to feel that works of art were literally going to kill me, there and then. I decided to go to Africa, to the Sudan. ... I came back to Britain completely changed, and I was never able to focus on Sotheby's again.' Working intermittently as a journalist for the next few years, he walked through Patagonia in the hope of writing a series of articles. But it was the resultant book *In Patagonia* which helped restore travel writing to its former prestige.

Colin Thubron started work in publishing and left to follow a life of travel, making television documentary films and writing five books about the Middle East. His book *Behind the Wall* is an account of a journey through China, ranging from the Burmese frontier to the Gobi Desert, from the Yellow Sea to the edge of Tibet – 'a brilliant mosaic of scenes and encounters including a tour of a mental hospital in Shanghai, a night in Mao's bed and a visit to a tongue doctor', as the citation read when he was awarded a Thomas Cook Travel Book Award.

Dervla Murphy had a very sheltered background before she took to travel writing on such an adventurous scale. Born in County Waterford, the daughter of the County Librarian, she had a convent education and then nursed her invalid mother until, in 1963, she was free to take her epic bicycle journey all the way from Ireland to India, a journey recounted in her book *Full Tilt*.

When Patrick Marnham won a Thomas Cook Travel Book Award for his book *So Far from God*, the story of his journey from Spain to Central America, the judges commented: 'Patrick Marnham's writing gives a vivid sense of place and awareness of the political climate of the countries he is travelling through. His journey is told with a breadth of understanding coupled with a sense of humour rare in travel books.'

Many writers graduate to travel writing from other forms of writing and journalism and can support themselves through other writing commissions; Patrick Marnham, for instance, was commissioned to tour West Africa to write a report on the Nomads of the Sahel for the Minority Rights Group.

Agents and publishers

There is constant discussion amongst writers about the pros and cons of having an agent. Briefly, agents take a 10% commission, negotiate contracts, particularly useful if your book is being sold overseas, and their knowledge of the market can save you considerable time and effort over which publisher to send you ms to. One drawback with agents is that they will only handle books and not journalism, so you still have to market your own articles.

The biggest problem with agents, however, is getting one in the first place. It is easy enough once you are established or have made your name – even one made in a totally different field – to get an agent, but in the beginning it is probably no more difficult to interest a publisher than to convince an agent that you will be worth acting for.

The *Writers' & Artists' Yearbook* and *The Writer's Handbook* are the most useful books to consult for the names of publishers and the types of book they publish. Strangely enough, many people don't appear to realise that publishers specialise in certain types of books, and manuscripts appropriate only to Mills & Boon keep pouring in to academic publishers, and academic subjects to publishers of erotic fiction.

Rather than send in your complete manuscript, it is better to start with a covering letter and a synopsis (plus postage for its return). Publishers of travel books include A & C Black, Reardon, Pavilion, Collins, Nicholson, Countryside Books, John Murray and Moorland. Supplement this list by studying the travel and guide books in your library or local book shop.

Don't however, make the mistake of compiling a list of publishers interested in travel books and, starting with number one on your list, post off your manuscript hoping for a favourable reply in a few month's time. Publishers tend to concentrate on their own specialised subjects, and travel is a very wide field. Although A & C Black, John Murray and Countryside Books all publish travel books, your book may be totally unsuitable for all three.

A & C Black publish the *Blue Guides*, Countryside Books specialise in illustrated regional guides and John Murray has published travellers and explorers from David Livingstone and Bates of the Amazon to Isabella Bird and Freya Stark. If the book you propose is a guide to the French canals and places en route where you will find the best meals, then it is obviously a waste of time sending it to any of the above publishers. Similarly, be realistic about whether your subject matter is paperback or hardback material. Narrative travel books usually appear in hardback and guide books frequently in paperback.

Public Lending Rights

If you are successful, and your book is published, then in all probability you will receive money from a source which, until the 1980s wasn't available to authors – Public Lending Rights.

Under this system, authors whose books are lent out from public libraries receive a payment once a year from public funds. The amount each author receives is in proportion to the number of times the book was lent out during the previous year, with a top limit of £6000 per author.

To participate, you must register the title and date of publication of your book, your name must be on the book's title page, and you must be resident in the UK (which, as far as PLR is concerned, doesn't include the Channel Islands or the Isle of Man), or Germany.

You can only be registered for Public Lending Rights if you apply during your lifetime (i.e. your heirs can't register your books after your death). Having registered, however, the PLR in your book or books continues until fifty years after your death. You are eligible for PLR as an author even if you don't own the copyright – PLR and copyright are different.

The number of times a book was lent out during the year is determined from a representative sample from twenty public libraries spread throughout England, Scotland, Wales and Northern Ireland, and multiplied in proportion to total library lending throughout the country. PLR applies equally to guide books as well as travel books, of course – every book, in fact, hardback or paperback, loaned over the counter in a public library. If your book is kept in the reference section, then unfortunately it doesn't qualify for PLR.

The sum allocated by Parliament for PLR amounts to several millions. After paying administrative costs, the remaining money is distributed among the authors registered on the basis of a pence-per-loan figure, which tends to vary each year according to the sum allocated and the number of authors registered.

You can get further details and application forms for PLR from The Registrar, PLR Office, Bayheath House, Prince Regent Street, Stockton-on-Tees, Cleveland, TS18 1DF, (telephone 01642–604699 or Fax 01642–615641).

8
Writing a Guide Book

Judging by the size of the annual Thomas Cook Travel and Guide Book awards, the narrative travel book is more highly rated than the guide book, for the top award for the former is three times that given to the latter. If it is any consolation, however, guide books are likely to be read and consulted by far more intending travellers, be bought in far greater numbers, and be borrowed from the local library more frequently than their autobiographical counterparts. Indeed Pausanias, who travelled in the second century AD, wrote a guide book to Greece that is still useful to this day, for he was writing at a time when many of that country's greatest monuments were still standing.

Guide books, in fact, have a long and honourable tradition, although Aldous Huxley was particularly scathing about guides written with an uncritical eye: 'For every traveller who has any taste of his own, the only useful guide book will be the one he himself has written. All others are an exasperation. They mark with asterisks the works of art which he finds dull, and they pass over in silence those which he admires. They make him travel long miles to see a mound of rubbish; they go into ecstasies over mere antiquity.'

Karl Baedeker published the first of his famous handbooks for travellers over 150 years ago, each one based on his personal observation and experience during his travels in that country. 'This tradition of writing a guidebook in the field rather than at an office desk has been maintained by Baedeker ever since', the publishers add, in case you imagined that guide books of such famous lineage would fail to up-date their guides at first hand once their founding father was no longer there to lead by example. Baedeker's *Russia* of 1914 claimed that its basic aim was 'to supply the traveller with as much information as will render him as nearly possible independent of hotel-keepers, commissionaries and guides, and thus enable him the more thoroughly to enjoy and appreciate the objects of interest he meets with on his tour', which, by and large, still holds true of guide books to this day, although most people are not averse to asking hotel-keepers for local information and some will positively court this.

In this country, A & C Black's long involvement with guide book publishing started with the publication of *Black's Economical Tourist of Scotland* in 1826, which was followed by more than fifty other titles by the 1890s, while John Murray's famous *Red Handbooks* go back to 1836, when the grandson of the founder wrote the very first one. By the end of the century Murray's *Red Handbooks* all but covered the known world and the publishers made the bold statement that 'some of the British passion for travel in the 19th century may well have been due to the success of the *Handbooks*'.

Charles Dickens published an *Unconventional Hand Book to London* over a hundred years ago and noted: 'The plan of a work of this character necessarily involves the mention of names; but every statement and every recommendation made in the Dictionary is put forth either as a result of actual experience, or on perfectly trustworthy authority', adding as a disclaimer: 'No payment has been received, or ever will be received, directly or indirectly, for anything that appears in the body of this book.'

The package tourist searching the shelves of the local library for a suitable guide to take on holiday may expect all guide books to be the same – basically a mix of essential information, where to go, how to get there and what to see. A little history perhaps, and topics like climate, tipping, shopping advice and some hotel and restaurant recommendations. Not a bit of it. Guide books come in as many varieties as soups.

Different types of guide book

There are guide books which look at a country in considerable detail, and guide books which only have room to cover the major cities and major sights. There are critical guide books and uncritical ones, some like those in the *Blue Guide* series which tend to be factual and impersonal and others such as the Rough Guides where the personality of the authors keeps breaking through.

David Benedictus, author of *The Essential Guide to London*, believes that 'the guide book which promotes the best without warning against the rest is no better than a travel agent who sells you tickets to a desert island paradise on a leaking boat, or who recommends a stretch of golden sands without mentioning the sharks who swim inshore and flash their shining teeth'.

Study the market

When the idea of writing a guide book first starts germinating in your mind it is a good idea to familiarise yourself with the various types of guides on the market first. It will be helpful not only in researching and writing your own book, but in researching a travel destination for your own benefit before embarking on a trip. Familiarity with the standard format and content of the best-known guides will help you find the type of information you need quickly. You may search through the erudite pages of the *Blue Guides* for information on archaeology and ancient sites, for instance, but you will search in vain for the addresses of night clubs.

A guide book is written for those who want to get ideas and information on what to see and do in a particular country or region, and although you may equally learn many useful facts from autobiographical travel books, it is not their *raison d'être*. Writing a guide book by no means excludes literary value but it does mean concentrating on what is important to your readers rather than concentrating on personal experiences (although the best guides tend to include both). In one of the *Travel Survival Guides* on Egypt and Sudan the author, Scott Wayne, tells how men and boys cloaked in gowns and turbans rush up to you in the streets of Khartoum and Kassala clutching swords, daggers and knives. 'When I arrived in Khartoum I didn't realise that these sword-bearing characters merely wanted to sell me their wares, so I ran away down the street the first time one of them waved his sword in my face.'

Blue Guides also give advice, but in a more objective and less ebullient manner. This passage describes visiting the pyramids at Giza:

> 'Many vendors offer camel and horse rides and this can be a very pleasant way to see the area. However, it is essential to ensure that your bargain with the dealer includes the return journey; unprepared visitors may find themselves with a couple of kilometres to walk back across the dunes.'

Guide books may well be written from start to finish by one person, but detailed guides frequently take the collaboration of many specialist writers to make publication within a specified time feasible. The up-market *In-World Guide*, aimed at enlightening millionaires and those still aspiring to the title on the hotels, restaurants and night-spots throughout the world in which they should be seen, has freelance correspondents throughout the world, each contributing a city profile. *The Economist Business Traveller's Guides* series had no less than twenty-two contributors, all experts in their field, for its *Germany on Business* title.

As the editor of the *Penguin Travel Guides* rightly claimed:

> It is hardly possible for any single travel writer to physically visit a thousand restaurants (and nearly that number of hotels) in any given year and provide accurate appraisals of each. And even if it were physically possible for one human to get through such an itinerary in a single year, it would of necessity have to be done at a dead sprint, and the perceptions derived therefrom would probably be even less valid than those of any leisurely layman visiting the same establishments.

Instead of a few travel writers running themselves ragged round the country, he prefers to recruit informed local correspondents and believes that they are much more likely to uncover 'hard-to-locate gems that so often turn an ordinary visit into an exciting adventure'.

The planning stage

If the travel book in your head is a literary one, a personal account of a journey through a foreign country, then it is relatively easy to sit down at the typewriter or word-processor and write a draft account more or less as it happened – the motivation for the book, the preparations you had to make, the people you met from A to B, the adventures you experienced on your way to C, how you were imprisoned at X and your camel died at Y. If all goes well, your book almost writes itself as experience crowds on experience.

Not so guide book writers, however. They have to sit down and plan. Routes, itinerary, how long to stay in each place. They have to allow time for note-taking, note-organising, time for research, time for writing. Without experience to guide you, is it better to write as you travel or to make extensive notes and write up the book at home, with the attendant risks of missing some all-important detail? To go back again and find out at first hand may be too costly in terms of money and time. Rain and thunderstorms may upset your schedule or make photography impossible – not a serious problem if you are writing a guide to the villages in your home county, but an expensive headache if you are writing a guide to Turkey, to Scandinavia, or to a notably expensive city like Tokyo.

Writing a guide involves reading every morsel of information you come across about the area, not only to discover everything worth seeing in the town/city/area which you are writing about, but for every hint of literary connections or a mystery which you can investigate when you are there and perhaps develop. There is no point in regurgitating other people's research secondhand; you must obviously find out as much new material for yourself as possible, adding your own dimension to your subject. The research you do at home before you start out is to help you plan your itinerary as a preliminary to writing the book.

Establishing the parameters

But first, establish the parameters of your book. Do you aim to write a guide book about a particular country, a region or perhaps a local guide covering your county? Who is your book intended for? For Brits travelling abroad to Greece, to Turkey, perhaps, or to the USA? For overseas visitors coming to Britain? Or do you want to write a guide book extolling the virtues and scenery, the wildlife and countryside of the shire where you live, which will interest people from other areas of the UK?

More particularly, who is it aimed at? The expense-account businessman who wants hotels with fax machines and where he can rely on getting a wake-up call each morning, or hard-up students who are prepared to sleep on a beach if necessary and rely on hitch-hiking to get from place to place?

Age and financial status are major criteria in deciding what type of information your guide book should contain, and are often inter-related. There are guide books aimed at the well-to-do traveller such as Louise Nicholson's *India in Luxury* and guide books such as the *Rough Guides* aimed at younger, less affluent travellers. Both are recommendable because of the integrity of the writing and descriptions, which does not depend merely on naming the nearest de-luxe hotel or the nearest youth hostel.

But you will have to define your market still further. How will your readers travel, for instance? Is it aimed at the reader who walks from A to B, or the motorist? Perhaps your ambition is to write a guide book for small boat owners, for hikers, those who spend their weekends on canals, or for cyclists. Will you include places en route where they can enjoy a good meal or a pub lunch in picturesque surroundings?

Will you include itineraries? Maps? Sketches? Will your publisher pay for these to be specially drawn or will you be expected to prepare them yourself, or pay for an artist to prepare them for you out of your advance? Will your guide contain photographs? If so, in colour or black and white? Again, will these be provided by the publisher or by you?

Are there already many guides in existence on your chosen subject? If so, can you add a new angle which will make it of interest to a publisher? Hundreds of guide books are currently available on London alone; almost every conceivable angle has been explored and written about, from *Royal London, Children's London, London for Americans, London for Free, London for the Disabled, London from the Air* and *Subterranean London*, but each year still more authors seem to find highly original angles to write about.

Remember that in addition to publishers' output, there are specialised guide books commissioned by the various tourist authorities which may already cover your particular approach, and there are also guide books sponsored in the main by car manufacturers. There is, of course, nothing to stop you from writing to a company suggesting they sponsor a guide book on your proposed theme, provided it is also within the scope of their interests, but the approach – of which it must be said they get many – more usually comes from a public relations company.

You may have absolutely no intention of writing a guide book when an invitation comes out of the blue: a situation that often arises when you least expect it, particularly if you have a reputation as an expert on a particular part of the world, or an article on this very subject has just appeared over your name in one of the nationals. The subject matter may be New York or the area within a fifty mile radius of where you live, but flattering as it is to be asked, never underestimate the time or effort involved in research, let alone in the actual compilation.

The pros and cons

Checking and rechecking facts is essential, but is a tedious chore and one that not everyone is temperamentally suited to. There is a world of difference between writing 500-word articles and embarking on a guide book which may run to 50,000 words.

On the other hand, you are not writing 50,000 words straight off on the one topic: the same subject matter certainly, but divided into chapters covering different aspects, many of which are already familiar to you. And if your invitation to write a guide book arose in the first place from articles you have already published, you are not starting completely from scratch.

But an invitation may have strings attached in that many guides form part of a series and must conform to a standard format. This has decided advantages, not least that you know what is involved before embarking on the project, the number of words required, the length of each chapter. The disadvantages for free spirits are that you may feel constrained and unable to arrange the format to your preferred pattern, which defeats your efforts to do your own thing.

You may well find that the publisher's art editor, if there is one, dictates the pace; captions of exactly 45 words, no more, no less. Hyphenated words may be thrown out if they spoil the look of the layout and the writer has to have a rethink. Writing text under such constraints cripples the creative side of writing; unless the rewards are particularly good, remember that you will seldom be adequately compensated for all the time you have spent cutting, expanding and revising.

Usually, though, the writer is left to his or her own devices. Here the problems may come from another direction – you may be pressurised by the artist drawing the maps or sketches. While his deadline may be exactly the same as the one you have been given, his other work and commitments may mean that the only time he can possibly devote to your maps is next week. And all this before you have even worked out your own itinerary . . .

Shaping your guide book

If you don't have to conform to a standard format, you will first have to decide on how to arrange your guide to give it shape; with a county guide it is often easier to concentrate on the towns and radiate from there to the surrounding areas of interest.

On the other hand, you may find it easier to compile the material in gazetteer-style, such as the *Shell Guides* or many of the *AA Guides*, or to concentrate on an itinerary that will take the walker or the motorist through the most interesting routes in a day or half-day. The aim is to get each chapter of equal interest, and problems come when you have the book's skeleton assembled and find that some places are overflowing with stately homes and castles, fine buildings, unusual shops and plenty of diversions, while others have only one or two major attractions to recommend them, and are centred in a mundane town.

The preparation of a guide book, so simple at first sight, frequently leads to your finding that the shape you first envisaged is unworkable. One, two or even several rethinks at this stage can save many frustrating hours and miles later on, when you suddenly realise that your original format is not going to work.

If you are taking your own photographs for the book, remember that the weather may be uncooperative and your arrival at a little-known historic house may coincide with a thunderstorm; do you stay in the area for another day hoping for better weather, plan to return at a later date or give up all hope of taking photographs?

More than once on press trips I have found that the isolated but very special church which was to have been opened specially for our party was shut and the person in charge of the key failed to turn up. Obviously an omission such as this in a short article is sad but not serious, but the guide book writer can't afford to ignore any building of interest or significance, and has to make a return visit if this kind of problem arises.

It is very necessary to keep in mind Robert Burns' advice that the best-laid schemes 'gang aft agley' and build in time for unforeseen circumstances between researching and writing up your notes, or between writing the final copy and delivering the manuscript to the publisher. A special return visit may have to be fitted in and if you haven't allowed sufficient time (and there hardly ever is sufficient time), you multiply your problems.

If you are writing a local guide book which will involve mention of National Trust properties, stately homes and gardens of that ilk, remember that, apart from the large, important properties such as Chatsworth House, Blenheim Palace and Woburn Abbey, many are open only from Easter until late September or October. So unless you know the house or stately home backwards your research trips will be dictated by many factors which will be outside your control. It is no use signing a contract in October for a guide book whose manuscript has to be delivered to the publishers in April if your research trips are likely to be rewarded by doors which are firmly shut and entertainments and theme parks which are closed for the winter. If you are the author, then as far as possible you must try to see and experience everything you mention at first hand.

Keeping pace with changes

But one of the chief headaches in writing a guide book stems from the rapidity with which, as a genre, they go out of date: they date even as they are being written and they date even more as they are being printed. Given that it can easily take up to a year to research and write a guide book, possibly more where the subject matter is specialised or involved, or when the country you are describing in great detail is not on your doorstep, the research may even take several years to accomplish. Printing the book takes a further few months, particularly in the case of a guide book rich in detail, maps, footnotes and colour photographs.

Given this time-scale between conception and birth, it may take 18 months before your guide book reaches the book shops. As those who live in what appear to be the most timeless of villages will know, a lot of changes can occur in two years, while material about a city such as London needs constant updating.

Most guide books are not updated each year and there may well be intervals of several years before the publishers get around to revising either the entire book or a particular section. Some publishers whose ambitious guide books embrace the cities of the entire world have a policy of updating their guides on a revolving basis, rather than revising and resetting the guide every year. At any given time, the chapter devoted to New York may have been completely revised, the chapter on London be a year old, the chapter on Berlin two. The following year, Berlin will be updated and by then London will be two years old and – especially in today's climate – getting very out of date.

Restaurant and hotel information is particularly vulnerable to change – London's famous Dorchester Hotel in Park Lane has changed hands more often in recent years than Park Lane in a game of Monopoly.

Famous buildings may crumble, and visitors no longer be admitted within the circle at Stonehenge, for example, but this is a hazard of travel. If the Leaning Tower of Pisa suddenly keels over one day, then it will be front page news and one hopes the reader will appreciate that guide books can hardly be up-dated immediately to take account of this catastrophe.

What you can do, however, is ensure that your facts are correct right up to the very day you hand your manuscript to the publisher. Accept philosophically that writing a guide book is a bit like painting the Forth Bridge and that some of the information you give will have changed before the book is in print.

Putting it all together

And when you are back home, surrounded by all the notes and photographs you have taken en route, what then? Only you know how quickly you can write, how many drafts you will have to make. Writing a guide book not only takes extraordinary patience, it takes extraordinarily good organisation and is invariably fraught with decisions on what to include and what to leave out. Remember, too, that unless you are a hobby writer, and content to write a travel guide for the good of your ego rather than the good of your wallet, you will still have to find time for your regular writing commitments, since the rewards of writing a travel book are unlikely to pay for your mortgage and living expenses.

It all makes you empathise with – but hopefully not emulate –
Arnold Toynbee, who remarked about his book on the industrial
revolution in England, 'When I had got all my notes written up, I
thought I'd polish it off in two summers. It took me 27 years.'

9
Taking Photographs: Help or hindrance?

Having suitable photographs to illustrate your travel articles is undoubtedly helpful when submitting travel features. Readers' eyes are invariably drawn to the illustrations first and if they are attracted by what they see, go on to read the article. One good photograph can encapsulate all you have said in a 500 word article, and even an average one complementing the article is better than none at all. Conversely, a gloomy picture of people dressed in macs looking round Northumberland ruins in the rain with their umbrellas up (and I have seen just such a one in the travel pages of a national newspaper) is totally offputting: I suspect the majority of readers didn't go on to read the article.

Editors are usually pleased to see photographs accompanying your article, provided they are of publishable quality. In the case of black and white this means not less than 5 × 7 inches, glossy, in focus, with clear, sharp images and good contrast. Needless to say, they should be germane to the article. It saves the editor considerable time phoning round the photo agencies, which in any case may not have an up-to-date photograph of the particular statue, beach or building you have mentioned in your article.

Photo libraries tend to specialise in certain subjects, but even those which specialise in travel cannot hope to cover every country in the world, let alone every island, every beach, every castle or every mosque. Some specialise in the Far East, some in the Caribbean, others in America, but their photographs may be out-of-date, especially when photographers haven't been back recently and a new bridge has completely altered the appearance of the landscape or a prominent building has been demolished to make way for a new motorway.

Selling through photo agencies

Many people have progressed into travel writing through photography. If you have built up a sufficient portfolio of travel photographs, and they are good enough, then a photo agency will handle them for you, include them in their library and take a percentage of the reproduction fee for any published. You retain the rights to your own work and 'lease' the photographs to clients. By the time you have thousands of pictures in stock the fees they generate should provide you with a steady income.

Taking your own pictures – the pros and cons

On the plus side, therefore, photography gives you the chance to capture the unfamiliar with a fresh eye, and there is little doubt that photographs accompanying your article will earn you extra money. On the negative side, many writers find that taking photographs other than for their own pleasure is distracting. They prefer to observe the world around them through their own eyes rather than the eye of the camera. They also find that concentrating on camera angles makes them deaf to sounds around them; they have photographs to show for the time they spent in the temple gardens but cannot recall whether there was bird song or silence. One journalist describes it as 'having to put your senses on the back burner while you concentrate on getting the light and the angle right'.

Landscapes can be the trickiest and least rewarding photographs you are likely to take, yet travel writers invariably feel a compulsion to film distant mountain ranges and coastlines misty with sea spray, because they feel this is what editors want. Even when conditions are perfect the results are so often disappointing in relation to the real thing.

Beware, too, of the lemming instinct which overtakes travel writers on tour buses which stop off at well-known beauty spots to allow passengers to admire the view. As everyone else rushes off the bus to take photographs, you are apt to feel a compulsion to take them too. But photographing such places needs a special eye for composition – a foreground object to focus readers' attention and lead them on to more distant objects, and if your landscape pictures are consistently disappointing then perhaps it is better to realise your limitations and concentrate on what you *are* good at.

Follow a theme

Ask yourself what kind of pictures you want to take rather than just shooting everything on sight. Having a theme such as children, markets, flowers or local crafts or industries such as rug weaving in Sardinia, batik production in Indonesia, or the tapestry weaving workshops near the pyramids of Cairo, helps to concentrate the mind and build up a stock library of specialised rather than general interest photographs.

Study the colour photographs in the pocket-sized *Berlitz Travel Guide* series. Although the *Guides* vary and some are better than others, the best contain pictures which are colourful, lively and original – all the qualities, in fact, that an editor looks for in travel photographs.

Black and white or colour?

Professional travel photographers carry a considerable weight of equipment round with them and even for unprofessional photographers, two camera bodies, one with black and white film, the other with colour, are almost mandatory if you have assignments for magazines as well as newspapers.

The increasing sophistication of cameras, however, means that almost everyone can take clear and expressive photos with one of the 35mm autofocus single-lens cameras on the market nowadays. For the aspiring photo-journalist, the simpler the equipment the better, and 35mm transparencies are perfectly acceptable for reproduction in most magazines. Although colour prints can be reproduced very satisfactorily in magazines using good coated paper, the preference is always for colour transparencies. A telephoto lens is a definite plus as it allows you to take close-ups of things such as gargoyles, statues, birds and animals which would otherwise be out of reach., but many 35mm compact cameras have a built-in zoom nowadays, making a separate one superfluous for most travel writers.

If you write mainly for newspapers, or have them in mind as your target market, use black and white film. Remember, however, that unless you are doing your own processing, it may take as long as seven working days to get the film developed on your return, unlike colour prints which your local chemist will turn round in 24 hours. If you have a large number of black and white films to be developed on a regular basis it may be worth while coming to an arrangement with your nearest processing house to see if you can get a faster turn round for your B/W photos.

Remember to jot down in your notebook the opening and closing scene of each roll and identify any particular sites you may have difficulty remembering later. If you aim to develop the photography side, and your camera isn't an automatic one, mark down details of exposure, light, distance etc., which, when you see the results, will be the best way of learning from your mistakes or improving on the results next time.

Be sure to take along sufficient quantities of film. Film is expensive, and the processing costs are high, but in relation to the cost of your trip to China, to Peru or Alaska – some of the places you may well find yourself in while writing about travel – it is cheap.

Kodak will help you if you are doubtful about what equipment and film you should take for filming in specific countries and conditions. One of their major concerns is that travel photographers should keep their films as cool as possible – not the easiest thing to achieve when you are bumping across the Sahara desert in a jeep. They also advise asking for a visual check of unprocessed films at airports, since the X-rays used by some security equipment can fog films.

What to concentrate on

What are the best subjects to photograph? Obviously you should shoot any scene which appeals to you in particular, but photographs of people – particularly characterful old people and young children, and especially if they are absorbed in something like hauling in fishing nets, playing games, riding a donkey, or making lace – are always saleable. Avoid having them look straight at the camera if at all possible. Market stalls, particularly food stalls, old women squatting on the ground behind half-a-dozen apples they are hoping to sell, pumpkins drying in the sun in America, vast dishes of paella being prepared in Andalucia, mounds of spices in a Turkish bazaar, Russian school-children in their uniforms and busy waterfront scenes enhance the travel angle with human interest.

Homework helps

It helps to have done some homework before a trip and know what to expect, so that you can take photographs at every stage of the story, and be at the right place at the right time. The divers at Acapulco, for instance, don't just jump from the cliffs straight into the rock-lined waters of the inlet below: they bless themselves first at a shrine, something easily missed in your anxiety to capture the divers' heart-stopping arc through the air, especially at night when they have flaming torches in their hands.

Unless you are a professional photographer, avoid the conventional shots of buildings that are the clichés of the travel world. If you must take them, try to photograph the buildings from an unusual angle or level (it must be said, though, that shots of the

Eiffel Tower from every conceivable angle fill UK photo libraries). But then even Paris in the spring, filled with young lovers, has become a cliché. Seeing a country from a fresh angle is no easier for the photographer than the travel writer, and serendipity plays no small part. I was lucky enough to be outside the cathedral in Lima when the local plumbers and electricians were gathering in the hope of being hired by passers-by. The resultant photograph proved much more popular than a conventional shot of the cathedral exterior.

Professional photographers never seem to photograph their own thumbs, cut off the top of people's heads, or have plants apparently sprouting from grandma's hair. These elementary mistakes usually happen through inexperience, and it is helpful to go to evening classes or weekend courses to learn how to make the best use of your camera

In my own area, which I imagine is pretty typical of the type of evening classes held throughout the country, there are currently five different courses, ranging from an introduction to the camera to the artistic side of photography, including composition, the effects of light, tone, pattern, texture and colour; outdoor photography and a course on close-up work and portraiture.

Professional tips

But even if you are confident and competent at using your camera you may find you are still not producing the type of photographs that editors will buy. Although I can't give advice on camera equipment and the type of lenses which ensure that everyone sunbathing on a beach appears to have an all-over tan, I can pass on some of the tips which professional travel photographers with whom I have travelled throughout the world have given me. Remember, however, that although you can be taught how to use the camera, taught how to look at things, in the end you are on your own.

The first tip improved my shots immeasurably yet was extremely simple. Remember those head-to-toe photographs of members of your family posed stiffly against a local landmark, seemingly miles from the camera? Remember the bed of flowers that looked so effective in the distance but was disappointing when the film was developed? Wrong! Get as close to your subject as possible so that it – be it a person or an object – fills the frame. Moving in as closely as you can with your camera will help you capture the full beauty of an exotic flower, as a glance at any of the bulb or seed catalogues will show.

Vary the angle. Most people take pictures standing up. Professional photographers lie on their stomachs, stand on ladders, climb trees, hang from bridges – anything to give them a different, more unusual perspective.

Keep your background as simple as you can or blur it out altogether. A fussy background detracts from the foreground, where the story is.

Try to photograph people walking into the camera rather than walking out into the distance.

Take pictures of signs to help you identify the places you visit.

Don't shoot into the sun – it causes flaring.

When you're taking a portrait shot focus on the subject's eyes and choose a plain background.

Choose your viewpoint so that lighting comes from one side. This helps to make the texture and features of buildings stand out.

Use overhanging branches, or an archway, fence or awning to provide a natural frame to your photographs when filming landscapes.

If it rains, don't put away your camera. Just look out for colourful subjects such as a bright umbrella or raincoat to create an eye-catching centre of interest. Otherwise concentrate on indoor shots on bad days.

Vary the type of photographs you take. Silhouettes are effective – palm trees, sombreros etc. Shadows can be effective – take shots of the shadow of a camel moving through the desert as well as a conventional close-up. City nightlife gives exciting photo opportunities. Street fairs and carnivals are good, particularly if filmed from a vantage point high above a crowd of spectators. And photographing at night produces some notably dramatic results. There may well be fewer tourists around a famous site late in the evening, which also helps.

Look for details. Rather than try to encapsulate the entire scene, concentrate on just one decorative element. A close-up of an ornamental detail (a door knob for instance), can be more interesting than a shot of the entire door. In a crowd, concentrate on one face which stands out rather than shoot a crowd scene.

Look out for signs that are humorous or typify the local flavour. Film someone wearing a T-shirt which identifies the destination. The Virgin Islands have a particularly good line in suggestive T-shirts.

A very successful American travel photographer always believes in 'putting a heart-beat' in her photographs – if she can't include a human being she will try to get a bird or animal in the photograph to give life to the picture.

There are certain laws taught in schools of photography, such as never putting the horizon line in the middle of the frame and not placing your key point of interest in the centre of the frame. You may know all the rules but prefer to ignore them; it takes time, though, to develop your own style.

Try to take shots of the unexpected. America's *National Geographic Magazine* relies more on photographs than on text and aims to have photographs that say it all in one shot, not four or five. Out of 16,000 transparencies recently shot on a four month assignment by one of their photographers he hoped 20 would eventually appear. As it happened, none at all were used – the article was killed, condemned by the editor as 'too predictable – you knew what was going to happen next'. In the end, it is originality which counts, not the quantity of material, which is a relief to travel writers who take only a modest number of photographs to illustrate their articles rather than aspire to be a travel photographer. In general, most photographers are not writers, most writers are not photographers, although there are quite a number of husband and wife 'teams' around where one does the writing while the other concentrates on the photography.

Courtesy points

If you encounter a colourful local character, it is always courteous to ask permission first before you take a photograph. Sending a copy of the photograph once it is developed is a kind gesture but may be impossibly time-consuming, especially if you have photographed someone who is illiterate and can't write out their name and address without the assistance of a friend. A few coins in their hand may be a happier solution. Some street-wise characters state their fee before they agree to pose for photographs.

Things to avoid

Be careful about the people you include in your photographs. High fashion clothes and extravagant hemlines will make your pictures look dated as soon as fashions change. A really good photograph can be sold time and time again so it pays to ensure that there are as few give-aways of the year it was taken as possible.

The locals who – consciously or unconsciously – model for you, should reflect the readership of the magazine you intend sending the article to. There is a world of difference between the 'models' you select if you intend sending the feature, say, to *E.T. (Executive Travel)* magazine as opposed to *The Lady*.

Different light conditions require different film speeds – make sure you buy the right film for your destination, particularly if you are going to a country in the Middle East, where the light is particularly strong. Take care, too, to have sufficient replacement batteries with you.

Photo presentation

Make sure your photographs are properly captioned and have your name and address on the back for their return. Don't be tempted to caption them in ink – for one thing the back of the photograph often won't take it without blurring, and the impression will show through on the other side. Either number the photographs and type corresponding captions on a separate sheet of paper, or type the captions separately and attach them to the back of the photographs with Sellotape or Cow gum. Make sure you send them out in an envelope with cardboard backing so that they don't get folded and creased en route. By all means put PHOTOGRAPHS – DO NOT BEND on the outside but don't expect the Post Office or the mail room of large companies to take much notice of it. If you are sending in your pictures on spec rather than on commission make sure you include a large self-addressed label with sufficient postage for their return.

Colour transparencies should be cardboard mounted, never glass, and sent in the clear plastic wallets which are sold for this purpose. Number them individually corresponding to the captions, which should be on a separate sheet of paper.

Free photo sources

If you aren't interested in taking photographs yourself, it is possible to acquire some to illustrate your article from various sources, the most common of which is the tourist office of the country you are writing about. If you can get them at source, so much the better, but, if not, most countries have opened offices in London. Unfortunately their selection is often very limited as, however good their photo library was to begin with, it has become depleted over the years as people return them in a mutilated state or omit to return them altogether. Publishers borrow them in large batches to illustrate their books and need to keep them for up to a year at a time. Unless your request coincides with the arrival of a new batch of photographs, the available choice may not exactly add sparkle to your article. Rather than send an inferior photograph, one that isn't sharp and interesting, don't send any at all.

Original colour transparencies are too expensive for most tourist offices to dole out, so cheaply-made duplicates are offered instead. If they aren't clear and colourful, or have even a hint of being slightly out of focus, it's better not to borrow them at all.

The photographs available from tourist offices are normally free, although you will have to sign a form promising to return them within a stated time and pay a nominal sum if they are lost or damaged.

Ironically, you will have to pay full picture agency fees if you borrow photographs from the British Tourist Authority or the English Tourist Board to illustrate an article which may well be extolling the beauties of your native heath. A request to borrow photographs from one of the local tourist boards often meets with a positive response, however, and at the moment these are free, but there is talk of charging at some point in the future – tourist boards vary from area to area in their ability or willingness to provide photographs and, like all photo libraries, will charge for any photographs lost or damaged. Although one can see their point, travel writers themselves are very much in the hands of the publication to which they have submitted the article and illustrations. Although most newspapers and magazines are punctilious about returning illustrations, there are many others which aren't so scrupulous, so in general think twice before you borrow photographs, particularly transparencies.

Public relations companies are a good source of free photographs, usually of excellent quality. If they don't handle their own public relations, tourist offices willingly give the names of PR companies working on their behalf. Make sure the photographs are all stamped Copyright Free, however (as all pictures taken for publicity purposes should be).

Tour operators such as Butlins (with their new Leisure Worlds), travel agencies, hotels (particularly the larger hotel groups), zoos, airlines and railways can usually be relied upon to supply bona fide travel writers with free photographs.

Beware of borrowing

Don't borrow photographs from a photo library, even though they may have the very photographs to illustrate your article. Not only will you be charged a holding fee – and remember the publication you send them to may hold them for months before publishing, even if they are suitable – you run the risk of having to pay the reproduction fees if they are used. Photographic libraries usually charge according to the size at which their pictures are reproduced

– even more if it makes the front cover – so if your chosen publication reproduces the photos you have borrowed as a whole page the resultant bill will far exceed the sum you receive for writing the article. Even six 35mm transparencies reproduced s/s (same size) at £40 a time will in all probability exceed your fee.

The moral is that if you can't provide your own pictures or borrow free ones, don't send any at all – leave it to the art editor of the paper or magazine to borrow them from the photo libraries themselves. That way they alone will be responsible for the reproduction fees.

10
Writing for the Overseas Market

Rumours of lucrative payments are constantly filtering through from America, making writers on this side of the Atlantic more than eager to tackle the US market. The rumours are not exaggerated – fees are often as much as ten times what you would be paid for a similar article in the UK press – but the competition is exceedingly keen. Although it is by no means impossible to get your articles published in the States, it is of enormous help to have contacts there. By and large, Americans find it difficult to write letters and prefer to pick up the phone and commission an article there and then as the notion takes them. If they don't know you exist, they can't call you for an article.

But the overseas market doesn't begin and end with America, and although the English-speaking markets of the USA, Canada, South Africa, Australia and New Zealand are an obvious target it is surprising how many newspapers and magazines are still published in English in countries forming part of the Commonwealth – Malaysia's *New Straits Times* and *Malay Mail*, for instance, *The Times of India* and Malta's *Times*.

There are numerous magazines published throughout the world for British expatriates and magazines such as *TNT* are published in London for Australian and New Zealand expatriates. All are interested in travel in the UK, where to go and how to get there.

In-flight magazines

Airline magazines are frequently published in English as well as the language of the country in which the airline originates. Gulf Air's *Golden Falcon* magazine is published in English and Arabic, and *Ronda*, the in-flight magazine of Spain's national airline Iberia is published in English as well as Spanish. Among the travel subjects which have been covered in its pages was one on The Cafés of Paris, an article which included such famous cafés as the Deux Magots, Fouquets, the Café de la Paix and Lipp. If you doubt this comes under the heading of travel writing, consider the truth of the sub-title: 'This is Paris, and in Paris, cafés are a trademark of the city; something that must be visited the same as the Louvre Museum or the Eiffel Tower.'

Almost every airline in the world, however tiny, likes to publish an in-flight magazine, although it often adds significantly to the airline's costs, not just in paper, printing and artwork, but in terms of the fuel needed to carry the extra weight. Titles vary from Kuwait's *Sunrise* and *Trade Winds* (Netherlands Antilles Airlines) to the enticingly named *Paradise* from the airline of Papua New Guinea, Air Niugini.

More accessible for British writers are the magazines published by British Airways, Aer Lingus, Virgin Atlantic Airways and Air UK, which are called *High Life, Cara, Hot Air* and *Flagship* respectively. Although most of the articles are commissioned, it's comparatively easy to get hold of copies and study their style and content. If you intend writing for an airline magazine – most of which are published by outside publishing houses rather than the airline itself – first establish which countries the airline flies to. Rare is the airline which will publish a travel article in its magazine on a destination which isn't on any of its routes.

Styles vary from the light and superficial, all right for a short island-hopping trip in the Caribbean where the scenery outside the window is much too diverting to ignore, to the more serious magazines published by airlines flying the Atlantic, when passengers can devote several hours to reading them. Charter flights ferrying holidaymakers to the sun have less serious editorial in their in-flight magazines than scheduled airlines carrying a high proportion of business travellers.

Market research

Finding overseas markets may need considerable research but the *Writers' & Artists' Yearbook* and *The Writer's Handbook* list some major markets and their requirements in Zimbabwe, Australia, New Zealand, Canada, Ireland and Northern Ireland as well as South Africa. The international edition of *Benn's Media* is usually available in the reference section of larger libraries and gives details of thousands of publications throughout the world, their addresses, circulation, and whether or not they are published in English. *Willing's Press Guide*, which should also be available in most libraries, gives the principal publications of Europe, the Americas, Australasia, the Far East, Africa and the Middle East. Many have London offices, but as these never deal with manuscripts always send yours direct to the publication.

It is possible to buy the American equivalents of our *Writers' & Artists' Yearbook* and *The Writers' Handbook* from Freelance Press Services, Cumberland House, Lissadel Street, Salford M6 6GG (0161-702 8225): the *Writer's Market* contains 4000 US markets; *The Writer's Handbook* has fewer markets but more on all aspects of free-lance writing. Both books are expensive compared to ours.

Submitting overseas

Although writing for American markets can be extremely lucra-tive, it is only so provided you meet with success, for you must enclose sufficient International Reply Coupons to pay for the return of your manuscript if it isn't suitable. If you include photographs and post by airmail – surface mail takes so long that a year can easily elapse before you get your MS back – your postage bill can run into pounds each time, especially when your manuscript may be returned through no fault of your own. A friend of mine once had his MS returned from America with the following note attached: 'We are sorry to return your MS but we cannot use it as the editor shot himself yesterday.' He is still wondering whether or not this was as a result of reading his article.

It is often better, and cheaper, to send a query letter first, perhaps with a copy of one or two pieces of your published work attached and, of course, International Reply Coupons. This doesn't guar-antee a reply, of course, since Americans aren't the best correspondents at any time, but it might help. If you have a word-processor it isn't necessary to get the rejected manuscript back as you can easily produce another top copy at the press of a button, but you may feel, like me, that getting it back is the only thread of contact you have with the publication, and even a rejection slip without any comments on it is better than no news at all.

The advice on studying your market holds good for overseas publications no less than British ones, but it must be admitted that everyone takes a chance now and then on sending an article over-seas to a publication they know only from the pages of *Writer's Market* or *The Writer's Handbook*. Occasionally it works, and great is the thrill of getting your first overseas acceptance.

Getting sample copies

Once you set your mind on writing for the overseas market – not just the American market but worldwide – it is surprising how many publications you can get 'samples' of. Friends and relatives overseas can be cajoled into sending copies of their newspapers; holiday-makers can be primed to buy local magazines for you (making sure they understand not to buy you the local version of publications such as the *Reader's Digest*), many South African and Australian publications have offices in London, Embassies and High Commissions frequently have libraries and reading rooms where back issues of their papers can be seen. Make sure all your friends know that you are interested in writing for overseas markets and ask them to keep any magazines they find on their travels – on boats and ferries, trains and airlines no less than in the country of their destination.

Although most newspapers have a maximum length of 800 words, American magazines carry much longer travel articles than British ones. It is not unusual for them to run to 3000–5000 words, whereas in Britain even half that amount would be an indulgence. If you send a query letter to an American publication you are quite likely to get a 'Guidance to Contributors' leaflet on their style, length and requirements in return.

Use your experiences for overseas markets too

Don't just look under the Travel and Holidays sections when you study *Benn's Media* and *The Writer's Market*. If you have a specialised subject such as caravanning or fishing, are the parent of a young child, or are a senior citizen, look for magazines under those categories as well. By and large our magazines here in Britain mirror those which are published in the USA, and if you intend to concentrate, say, on writing about the joys and tribulations of travelling with young children or your travel experiences as a businessman or as someone who has recently retired, then try some suggestions on corresponding US magazines.

At one end of the age spectrum are magazines such as *American Baby* and *Parents*, at the other well-known magazines such as *Modern Maturity* which is published by the American Association of Retired Persons and is aimed at the 55-year-old and upwards market. Don't overlook magazines like *Sports Illustrated* or *Modern Bride* with their specialised market (the latter carries travel articles centred round honeymoon destinations), and newspapers such as the *Los Angeles Times* with its special supplements on international travel, European travel, cruising, etc.

What should you write about?

What to write about? The things that overseas visitors are most interested in seeing when they visit the UK is perhaps the most obvious answer. Once you have established a steady link with an overseas connection it may be possible to suggest articles on destinations other than the UK, but initially they are more inclined to take articles about Britain from the British, articles on France from the French and features on Italy from someone with an Italian address.

What you write about also depends on the readership of the publication to which you are submitting the article. For magazines such as Condé Nast's *Traveler*, for instance, you can be sure that readers are more interested in country house hotels than youth hostels, that the *New York Times* has an audience akin to our own *Times* and will be interested in our stately homes and in our national parks and, unlike many papers and magazines published in the USA, be aware that there is a world beyond London, and a completely different one at that.

There are, however, certain subjects which have a broad appeal to most overseas publications from the up-market glossies to the down-market tabloids. One of them is where to go to spot Royalty – places such as the Isle of Wight during Cowes Week, polo at Windsor Great Park, Royal Ascot, and the Braemar Games. The style and treatment depends very much on the market, however, which makes it desirable to see copies of the publication you aim to submit the article to.

Now that the BBC and ITV are selling soaps like *Coronation Street* to the most unlikely corners of the globe, an obvious angle for the travel writer is to tie in an article with a TV series. The Yorkshire Dales, Jersey and Oxford have all been the setting of a popular film or television series and have noticed a significant increase in overseas tourists afterwards. But get a head start this time. Watch out for news of forthcoming films and series where the background is as important to the storyline as the stars – it may be centred round a place, a castle or coastline that is familiar to you, and which you can write about before everyone else gets to their word-processor.

Granada Studios took a lesson from the success of the Universal Studios Tour in Los Angeles and opened a multi-million tourist attraction adjacent to their TV Studios in Manchester. The tour takes in the set of Downing Street and the House of Commons which was made for the Jeffrey Archer series *First Among Equals*, Baker Street for *Sherlock Holmes* and, most famous of them all, the set for *Coronation Street* and the 'Rover's Return'.

Being a tourist is an exhausting business and overseas visitors might well be grateful for a spot of R & R (rest and recouperation) at one of our health farms before touring the rest of Europe.

There are major festivals such as Edinburgh and Aldeburgh to write about, but don't overlook the minor ones too – they may not have the international prestige of Edinburgh but nevertheless hold great significance for a niche market or be the hook for an article on a particular town or place you know well.

The changing seasons are a reason why people visit the UK. We may complain constantly about the weather, moan about the rain or the cold, but many overseas visitors come from countries which seldom have rain, never see snow, and where they live in searingly high temperatures without the relief of rain. No wonder that the sight of our green fields sends them into ecstasies. Think of all the possibilities our weather and seasons give the visitor accustomed to the constant humidity of Singapore or the searing heat of Arizona in summer, and draw up a list of suggestions. Why let Paris have all the tourists in spring? There are places in England adrift in apple blossom in spring time, autumn in the Highlands is breath-taking, and Christmas in one of our country inns is a beguiling idea. But take care to submit articles geared to the seasons at least 4–6 months in advance, particularly in the case of magazines.

Ethnic connections

The ethnic connection is another source of ideas when writing and marketing your travel articles overseas. The descendants of Scottish emigrants to Canada during the Highland Clearances (there are 55 pages of 'Macs' in the Toronto telephone directory alone), descendants of the Welsh miners who settled in Patagonia, the Irish who went to Boston, or the GI Brides who sailed from Southampton after the last war tend to dwell on their roots as they become older and show a growing interest in reading about places where their parents, grandparents and great-grandparents hailed from. Conversely, of course, if you have just returned from Boston or attended the Highland Games in Nova Scotia or even Dubai, your experiences might go down well in *The Irish Times* and *The Scotsman* respectively.

It doesn't just end with the American connection of course. The populations of Australia, New Zealand and South Africa are still significantly composed of the descendants of British emigrants, and although the composition is changing rapidly nowadays and the ties with the old country are being dissolved as the popula-tion melds together to assume a more cohesive national identity, nevertheless there is still a strong enough interest in the old country to be assured of a market for travel articles which ring the right note.

As in Canada in general (Nova Scotia in particular), the population of New Zealand's South Island has strong Scottish roots and associations.

Captain Cook discovered New Zealand and his history may be traced in Whitby, where his ship the *Endeavour* was built, and his birthplace, now a museum, at Marton, where the rare and beautiful plants like the hibiscus and bottlebrush, which the botanists who explored the Antipodes brought back with them, may be seen in bloom.

The American connection

It is not hard to seek American connections in Britain. There is a splendid American Museum at Claverton on the outskirts of Bath where you can eat brownies made to Martha Washington's recipe, see friendship quilts, and marvel at the bravery and endurance of the early settlers as they travelled west in their covered wagons. At Dorchester Abbey in Oxfordshire there is a stone corbel depicting the face of Bostonian Edith Stedman, carved as a gesture of appreciation for the help given towards restoration by the American Friends of Dorchester Abbey.

There are Anglo-American societies all over the UK helping with money and resources to keep up the fabric of our heritage. The Magna Carta Memorial in Runnymede, Surrey, close to the site of the memorial to the late John F. Kennedy, was the gift of the American Bar Association. Sometimes the heritage is not fact but fiction: there's an Anglo-American Lorna Doone Society which has its HQ in the Lorna Doone Centre in Dulverton.

Jersey has many real life connections with the USA, not least in Lily Langtry who was earning as much as £500 a week in America in the last century; Buffalo Bill, who was descended from a Jersey family by the name of Le Caudey; and in such famous name connections as New Jersey.

It is always a help to know something of American history before deciding where best to submit your article. Minnesota, a city on the northern banks of the Mississippi River, for instance, has strong German, Scandinavian and Irish influences, and keen musical interests, with regular festivals of British music. With its twin city of St Paul it also claims to have more theatres (104 in all) than any other American city except New York, and its inhabitants regularly see plays by British playwrights – Stoppard as well as Shakespeare, which suggests that they would be just as interested in travel articles on subjects like the Open Air Theatre in Regent's Park and Glyndebourne as in those with a 'back to one's roots' theme.

South-east England is alive with American connections, all of them attractive and easily visited from London. This is a plus with most overseas visitors, who are invariably based in the capital for some, if not all, of their stay in Britain. Places such as Hever Castle and Leeds Castle, both in Kent, for instance – the former was purchased and restored earlier this century by the American William Waldorf Astor, who later took British citizenship and became the first Viscount Astor of Hever.

Leeds Castle was owned by Lord Culpepper, Governor of Virginia in the 17th century, and his grandson, a lifelong friend of George Washington whom he first employed as a surveyor, was the only British peer to emigrate to the New World. The Virginian side of the family claimed the title in 1908 and thus an American took his seat in the House of Lords.

But don't go too far into the past for your material: Shakespeare, Robert Burns, Beatrix Potter and the Beatles have lured many a tourist to our country, but who and what will attract them here in the future? If you can find the answers, the overseas market may well be your personal oyster.

11
Meeting Other Writers

Would that we could all have the drive and determination (not to mention the ability) to sit down and write a book straight off the cuff. Unfortunately we are not all blessed with the creative energy of Jeffrey Archer or Jackie Collins, and to have the company and criticism of other writers often acts as a jump start when inspiration fails or rejection slips have dejected and discouraged you.

Where to find the company of other writers? The London Writer Circle is large enough to embrace monthly talks by noted authors and journalists (Rose Tremain, P.D. James, Beryl Bainbridge, etc.) in addition to separate article writing, poetry and short story groups which also meet on a monthly basis. There are thriving Writers' Circles in the suburbs although these don't, naturally, have the same clout when it comes to attracting famous speakers.

Outside major cities, the local library or community centre is the most likely place for Writers' Circles to meet. Staff at the library should be able to put you in touch with the secretary. Failing this, if you can't find a circle near you, put an ad in the local paper and start your own.

Apart from the supportive embrace of a Writers' Circle and the companionship of like-minded people, the feed-back on your work can be extremely helpful. The criticism can be as useful as the encouragement – writers are often too close to their own work to notice the obvious. The competitive spirit of many a Writers' Circle is alone a great incentive to carry on writing, on the basis of 'if Simon can get an article published in *The Sunday Times* then so can I.'

Another advantage of Writers' Circles is the sharing of information on new markets and – frequently – a shared subscription to the two magazines published for writers, *Writers' Monthly* and *Writers News*.

But it has to be admitted that many local circles are not the right scene for travel writers. Some dwell almost exclusively on poetry – often very good poetry – or concentrate on short stories, but if your genre is travel writing, or indeed article writing in any form, then the group is not for you. It is also a waste to belong to a group with no ambition to see its work in print, be it articles, fiction or non-fiction.

Writers' Circles are mainly for those who have already put pen to paper, but for those who have no history of writing, have always wanted to but don't know where to start, there are some excellent courses – variously entitled *Creative Writing, So You Always Wanted to Write, Writers' Workshops* etc – run by local authorities or further education colleges throughout the country. These will get you started on a small scale to begin with, so that by the end of the term or year you can tackle a variety of subjects with confidence and may even find yourself in print for the first time.

If you intend to specialise in travel writing, joining one of the specific courses at the colleges listed below helps to concentrate the mind on essentials. Mike Gerrard, whose travel articles regularly appear in the nationals and who is the author of several travel books, holds travel journalism courses at these colleges once a year and several of his students have subsequently gone on to sell travel articles to the *Guardian*, the *Independent* and the *Observer*:

The Earnley Concourse, Earnley, Chichester, West Sussex
    PO20 7JL. Tel. 01243–670392
West Dean College, nr Chichester, West Sussex PO18 0QZ.
    Tel. 01243–63301
Missenden Abbey, Gt Missenden, Bucks HP16 0BD.
    Tel. 01494–890296
Wensum Lodge, King Street, Norwich NR1 1QW.
    Tel. 01603–666021
Burton Manor College, South Wirral, L64 5SJ.
    Tel. 0151–336 5172
Urchfont Manor College, nr Devizes, Wilts SN10 4RG.
    Tel. 01380–840495

He also holds travel journalism courses at Millers House Hotel, Middleham, North Yorkshire Tel. 01969–22630. There are other travel writers lecturing throughout the country of course, but check on their current credits before signing up, and make sure they have experience of today's markets.

If there are no courses near you or you aren't a 'joiner', a subscription to *Writer's Monthly* (29 Turnpike Lane, London N8 0EP. Tel. 0181–342 8879 or *Writers News* which also incorporates *Writing Magazine* (PO Box 4, Nairn IV12 4HU) provides interest and stimulation about all forms of writing. Both include writing competitions on a given theme, though the latter favours short story competitions rather than any other kind.

12
Computer Speak

Gone like quill pens are the days of unevenly typed articles laboriously produced on ancient portables. You don't have to invest in a computer or word-processor but it makes the actual production of a manuscript quicker and easier, and will save you an enormous amount of time rewriting and resubmitting articles.

You can command the word-processor or computer to delete words, sentences and entire paragraphs or switch them to a different page. It will enable you to add in words and sentences without having to retype the article in its entirety. Many word-processors/computers will add up the number of words you have written and check your spelling. Even more useful, it will check through your manuscript and correct discrepancies in the spelling, ie Tokyo on one page and Tokio on another. Recent models have built-in fax and modem.

Mastering the various programs isn't easy and will almost certainly cause you angst, expletives and lost work to begin with as pages and chapters disappear down black holes. But it can also be a source of enormous interest and pleasure, with a very professional-looking manuscript at the end of the learning curve.

A lesson or two from an experienced word-processor operator is always worthwhile. The shop from which you bought your word processor should be able to give you the name of someone who will give you a day's tuition. Alternatively, many colleges of further education hold one-day teach-ins, often on a Saturday, which will be sufficient to give you the basics. Joining an evening class helps to improve your skills and gives you a teacher to turn to for advice when you encounter difficulties. At the rate of one lesson a week, however, progress is too slow if you have already bought a word-processor and are impatient to use it.

Unfortunately word-processors and computers pass their sell-buy date faster than fruit in a greengrocers. I was one of the first people to buy an Amstrad PCW, a dedicated word-processor that was sturdy, reliable, cheap and extremely easy to master. (A computer is more versatile in that it will also crunch numbers, but the real work is done by software). But things have moved on since I bought it. The Amstrad's 3″ disks are now incompatible as PC standard disks are 3½″. Increasingly publishers expect regular contributors to send in articles and book manuscripts on 3½″ disk, a point to bear in mind when contemplating a brilliant future in travel writing.

If there is one thing more confusing than mastering a new word-processor, it's finding out what type to buy in the first place, especially when you find yourself surrounded by dozens of more or less identical-looking models. The following acronyms and jargon may help you find your way through the computer-speak of advertisements and salesman. Bear in mind that there's always a new generation of chips coming along which will be faster and more powerful but not necessarily better for you as a writer. Before you shop around, write down all the 'ingredients' you want in your ideal word-processor/computer, such as a thesaurus or word count, and, most importantly, check that it is PC compatible and how much memory is supplied as standard.

BIT   Binary digit – electrical signal sent out by the microchip.

BOOT UP   The power switch is on and the computer is ready to start work.

BYTE   Unit of measurement. One byte is roughly equivalent to one character on the screen.

COMPATIBILITY   Some personal computers conform to recognised industry standards, others don't. The advantage of a PC-compatible (nowadays industry standard compatible) computer is that you have access to a wide choice of software and more versatility.

CPU   Central Processing Unit. The part of the PC that looks like a box.

CURSOR   The small flashing dot, square or line which shows where you are working on the screen.

DISK/DISC   The piece of equipment used to store or retrieve information. The disk drive is a simple slot on the side of the personal computer. Also see *Hard Disk*.

DOS   Disk Operating System. Microsoft invented the system, hence the oft-quoted MS-DOS.

HARD DISK   Disk built into the computer which stores or retrieves information as it spins. Performance is measured in terms of access time (less than 19 ms is ideal). Has a capacity running up to several hundred megabytes.

ICONS   The name for the on-screen symbols in some programs, eg a waste-paper basket.

MEGABYTE   One million bytes. A computer's memory power is usually measured in megabytes.

MEMORY   Where everything you're working on is remembered or stored. When you buy a personal computer check that it has enough memory for your needs. 4MB (megabytes) is more than sufficient for a lengthy book.

MHz   Short for Megahertz – the speed at which information moves through the processor.

MODEM   Acronym for Modulator/Demodulator. Gadget which enables you to send articles direct from one PC to another (e.g. from your personal computer to a newspaper office) down the telephone line.

PC   Personal Computer

MONITOR   The screen on which your work appears.

MOUSE   An alternative to using the keyboard. The name for the mouse-shaped device which controls the movement of the arrow on the screen and instructs your personal computer to perform various procedures.

RAM   Random Access Memory. Where everything you are working on is stored.

ROM   Read Only Memory. Area from which information can only be retrieved (ie not altered). Electronic version of a book but instead of turning the pages you use the mouse to 'read' the text.

WINDOWS   Operating system developed by Microsoft which uses menus, icons and windows, with a mouse.

If you don't want to get to grips with a computer but have been asked to submit work on disk, remember the old standby of using a secretarial agency. Most of these have kept up with the times and can produce work for you on disk as readily as on paper. Remember to stipulate that you want hard copy as well (ie a printed-out version so that you can check that there are no mistakes or inaccuracies on the disk).

Tourist Offices in the UK

Tourist offices are increasingly using 01891 numbers which means that the caller pays for the call. Check the current rate for these numbers before calling and bear in mind that it may take as long as 10 minutes to get the information you require.

Australia
Australian Tourist Commission, Gemini House, 10–18 Putney Hill, London SW15 6AA. Tel. 0181–780 1496

Austria
Austrian National Tourist Office, 30 St. George Street, London W1R OAL. Tel. 0171–629 0461

Bahamas
Bahamas Tourist Office, 10 Chesterfield Street, London W1X 8AH. Tel. 0171–629 5238

Barbados
Barbados Board of Tourism, 263 Tottenham Court Road, London W1P 9AA. Tel. 0171–636 9448

Belgium
Belgian Tourist Office, 29 Princes Street, London W1R 7RG. Tel. 0171–629 0230

Bermuda
Bermuda Tourism, 1 Church Road, London SW11 3LY. Tel. 0171–734 8813

Britain
British Tourist Authority, Thames Tower, Black's Road, London W6 9EL. Tel. 0181–846 9000

Bulgaria
Bulgarian National Tourist Office, 18 Princes Street, London W1R 7RE. Tel. 0171–499 6988

Canada
Canadian Tourist Office, Canadian High Commission, 1 Grosvenor Square, London W1X OAB. Tel. 0171–258 6596

China
China National Tourist Office, 4 Glentworth Street, London NW1 5PG. Tel. 0171–935 9427

Czech Republic
Embassy, 26 Kensington Palace Gardens, London W8 4QY Tel. 0171–727 9654

Denmark
169/173 Regent Street, London W1R 8PY. Tel. 0891–600109

Egypt
Egypt Tourism Office, 168 Piccadilly, London W1V 9DE. Tel. 0171–493 5282

England
English Tourist Board, Thames Tower, Black's Road, London W6 9EL. Tel. 0181–846 9000

Finland
Finnish Tourist Board, 30 Pall Mall, London SW1Y 5LP. Tel. 0171–930 5871

France
French Government Tourist Office, 178 Piccadilly, London W1V OAL. Tel. 0891–244 123

Germany
German National Tourist Office, 65 Curzon Street, London W1Y 7PE. Tel. 01891 600100

Greece
Greek National Tourist Organisation, 4 Conduit Street, London W1R 0DJ. Tel. 0171–734 5997

Hong Kong
Hong Kong Tourist Association, 125 Pall Mall, London SW1Y 5EA. Tel. 0171–930 4775

Hungary
Hungarian National Tourist Board, 15 Cotman Close, London SW15 6RG. Tel. 0181–788 3091

India
Government of India Tourist Office, 7 Cork Street, London W1X 2AB. Tel. 0171–437 3677

Ireland
Irish Tourist Board, Ireland House, 150 New Bond Street, London
W1Y OAQ. Tel. 0171–493 3201

Israel
Israel Government Tourist Office, 18 Great Marlborough Street,
London W1V 1AF. Tel. 0171–434 3651

Italy
Italian State Tourist Office (ENIT), 1 Princes Street, London W1R
8AY. Tel. 0171–408 1254

Jamaica
Jamaica Tourist Board, 2 Prince Consort Road, London SW7 2BZ.
Tel. 0171–224 0505

Japan
Japan National Tourist Organisation, 167 Regent Street, London
W1R 7FD. Tel. 0171–734 9638

Kenya
Kenya National Tourist Office, 25 Brook's Mews, London W1Y
1LG. Tel. 0171–355 3144

Luxembourg
Luxembourg National Tourist Office, 122 Regent Street, London
W1R 5FE. Tel. 0171–434 2800

Malaysia
Malaysia Tourism Board, 57 Trafalgar Square, London WC2N
5DU. Tel. 0171–930 7932

Malta
Malta National Tourist Office, Suite 300, Mappins House,
4 Winsley Street, London W1N 7AR. Tel. 0171–323 0506

Netherlands
Netherlands Board of Tourism, 25–28 Buckingham Gate, London
SW1E 6NT. Tel. 01891–200 277

New Zealand
New Zealand Tourism Board, New Zealand House, Haymarket,
London SW1Y 4TQ. Tel. 0171–973 0360

Norway
Norwegian Tourist Board, Charles House, 5 Lower Regent Street,
London SW1Y 4LR. Tel. 0171–839 6355

Poland
Polish National Tourist Office, 310 Regent Street, London W1R
5AJ. Tel. 0171–580 8811

Portugal
Portuguese National Tourist Office, 22 Sackville Street, London
W1X 1DE. Tel. 0171–494 1441

Scotland
Scottish Tourist Board, 23 Ravelson Terrace, Edinburgh EH4 3EU.
Tel. 0131–332 2433

Singapore
Singapore Tourist Promotion Board, 126–130 Regent Street,
London W1R 5FE. Tel. 0171–437 0033

South Africa
South Africa Tourism Board, Regency House, 5–6 Alt Grove,
Wimbledon, London SW19 4DZ. Tel. 0181–944 6646

Spain
Spanish National Tourist Office, 57–58 St. James's Street, London
SW1A 1LD. Tel. 0171–499 0901

Sweden
Swedish Tourist Board, 73 Welbeck Street, London W1N 8AN.
Tel. 0171–487 3135

Switzerland
Swiss National Tourist Office, Swiss Centre, New Coventry
Street, London W1V 8EE. Tel. 0171–734 1921

Thailand
Tourism Authority of Thailand, 49 Albemarle Street, London
W1X 3FE. Tel. 0171–499 7679

Turkey
Turkish Information Office, 1st Floor, 170–173 Piccadilly, London
W1V 9DD. Tel. 0171–734 8681

USA
US Travel & Tourism Administration, PO Box 1EN, London W1A
1EN. Tel. 0171–495 4466

Wales
Wales Tourist Board, Brunel House, 2 Fitzalan Road, Cardiff CF2
1UY Tel. 01222–499909

Index